Who Am I
In the Lives of Children?

An Introduction to Teaching Young Children

Stephanie Feeney
University of Hawaii

Doris Christensen
The Early School
Honolulu, Hawaii

CHARLES E. MERRILL PUBLISHING COMPANY
A Bell & Howell Company
Columbus   Toronto   London   Sydney

To students in the
Early Childhood Education Program
at the University of Hawaii, and to the
staff, parents, and children of The Early School.

PUBLISHED BY
Charles E. Merrill Publishing Company
A Bell & Howell Company
Columbus, Ohio 43216

This book was set in Schoolbook.
The Production Editor was Cynthia Donaldson.
The cover was prepared by Will Chenoweth.

Cover photograph courtesy of Thomas Scarlett III.
Photographs in this book were taken by Sally Gale.

International Standard Book Number:
0-675-8391-5

Library of Congress Catalog Card Number:
77-92935

3 4 5 6 7 8—82 81 80 79

Printed in the United States of America

Preface

This book is an introductory text for students who wish to become teachers of young children. In it, we focus on the personal and professional development of the teacher as well as offer information about child development and early childhood education programs.

Our goal is to help prospective teachers acquire the awareness, information, and skills that they need to become competent and nurturing teachers of young children. We also want to help students develop self-awareness and an individual philosophy and style of teaching.

The material in this book has been developed in the Early Childhood Education Program at the University of Hawaii over the last five years. The program is still very much in process. Our ideas about child development, early childhood education, and teacher education have changed over the years and have continued to develop. But while this book may not contain definitive answers, it does raise important issues and questions, and it points to productive ways of looking at children, at learning, and at ourselves.

A Comment about Gender

We realize that teachers and children come in both sexes. We tried, without success, to find a style of writing which reflected this fact and was not awkward and cumbersome. For ease of reading, we have decided to follow the current convention in early childhood literature and refer to the teacher as "she" and the child as "he."

Acknowledgments

We are deeply grateful for the contributions to our knowledge and to this book that have been made by our students, friends, and colleagues. There is no way that we can include everyone who has assisted us, but we would like to acknowledge some of the major contributions.

First, we want to express our very deep appreciation to our friend and colleague Jean Fargo. Without her, our program would not have evolved in the ways that it has, and this book would not have been written. Jean has shared her ideas generously and has helped us to apply them to our program. She has contributed to our emphasis on values as a central concern in defining oneself as a teacher and in designing programs for children, and to our approach for looking at systems of classroom management. She also played a major role in helping us conceptualize and write the chapter on working with parents. More important, Jean's enthusiasm, encouragement, commitment to excellence, and ability to generate and explore ideas have been a source of inspiration.

We are very grateful to the children, staff, and parents of The Early School in Honolulu, a truly caring community. We have learned a great deal from observing the growth of the school, its staff, and the children, and we have benefited from the opportunity to put many of our ideas into practice.

The dedication of this book reflects our gratitude to students in the Early Childhood Education Program at the University of Hawaii. They have been subjected to numerous versions of this material and have given us invaluable feedback by reacting to it. They also have been a constant source of support and encouragement.

Graduate students in Early Childhood Education at the University of Hawaii have been of great assistance in conceptualizing, writing, revising, and teaching the material presented in this book. We are very grateful to them and wish to acknowledge them, especially the contributions made by Francine

v

Cummings, Christine Jackson, Susan Magee, Eva Moravcik, Carol Phelps, and Christine Wetzel. Special thanks are offered to Mark Jeffers, who never let us lose sight of the process.

Mary Ann Lester played a very important role in the translation of our ideas into reality. She did much of the research and wrote the first drafts of Chapter 4, *History and Models,* and Chapter 7, *The Learning Environment.* We have also benefited from her review of our writing and her ability to ask just the right question to prod our thinking one step further.

We thank Laureen Fitzharris for allowing us to adapt portions of her master's thesis in Chapter 9, *Working with Parents.*

Our friends and colleagues have shared their experiences and ideas and have given us new insights with their responses to our work. Our thanks here go to Hannah Lou Bennett, Jackie Dudock, George Fargo, Paul Haygood, Tony Picard, Marion Magarick, Shirley Mayfield, and Anita Trubitt. We are especially grateful to Joe Murray, who convinced us that we *could* write this book, and to Fred Kinne, administrative editor at Charles E. Merrill Publishing Company, who had enough faith in us to make it a reality.

We are grateful to Bob Stanfield for his help in organizing our ideas and for his ability to bring focus and clarity to our writing through his editing skill. Many thanks also to Roger Whitlock for raising our consciousness about writing and for his assistance in editing.

The sensitive photographs of children and teachers were taken by Sally Gale at the Early School, the Kuapa School of the Kindergarten and Children's Aid Association, Tenrikyo Preschool, and the University of Hawaii Head Start Program. For these we owe Sally a great deal.

Finally, we wish to express our appreciation to Elsie Bow, Gerry Bridgman, and Sharon Bogue for typing the manuscript. Special thanks to Sharon for her patience and moral support.

S. F.
D. C.

Contents

*Who Am I
In the Lives of Children?*

An Introduction to Teaching Young Children

Introduction

This book grows out of our experience—as children and adults, as learners and teachers. Our childhood experiences in school were very different. Stephanie attended public schools in a large California city and remembers them as dreary places where little important learning took place. Doris attended a one-room school in rural Idaho and had, for the first six years of school, a teacher who truly cared for children. Her initial experiences in school were happy and positive.

Although our early school experiences were very different, we have as adults many of the same feelings and ideas about education. We have visited and worked in schools that were happy and productive places and schools that were mindless and destructive. We have met and worked with teachers who have been an inspiration to us in their ability to relate to and nurture children and teachers who seemed to stifle the natural exuberance of childhood.

In addition to being influenced by our firsthand experience, our ideas have been influenced by educators like John Holt, Sylvia Ashton-Warner, George Dennison, A. S. Neill, Bruno Bettelheim, and Fritz Redl, who have shared their feelings and insights about work with children through their writing. We have also been influenced by and will draw on the work in humanistic psychology of, Abraham Maslow, Carl Rogers, and Arthur Combs, and will draw both on their work and that of Jean Piaget, Erik Erikson, and others in child development.

Our experience and education have led us to believe that education should stress the development of humanness in children and should deal with all areas—social, emotional, and physical as well as intellectual—of a child's development. In short, we are interested in the development of the whole child.

As we wrote this book we looked forward to the day when you, the prospective teacher of young children, would open to this page. You will play an important part in the lives of the many children you will teach, and this book represents our efforts to find effective methods to enable you and students like you to understand preschool and kindergarten children and contribute to their growth.

There are many approaches to teaching college students to teach young children. Each college instructor has a different idea of what is right or best for young children and what constitutes desirable classroom practice. Often, however, prospective teachers are not given the guidance they need to discover what *they* value and what *they* want for children. As a result, they have little chance to develop their own philosophy and teaching style. The traditional approach to teaching students to teach is comparable to making a clay figure by forming the pieces—head, arms, legs—and sticking them onto the central core, the torso. Students in traditional programs are given many pieces, but often are not shown how to put them together. And like the clay figure made by the stick-on method, whose arms and legs may fall off when subjected to stress, a student may find herself inadequately prepared for what she finds when, as a new teacher, she enters a classroom filled with noisy, active children.

Our approach to teaching students to teach is like creating a clay figure in which each part is shaped from the central lump of clay. Such an approach, we have found, produces teachers whose teaching is an integral part and expression of who they are. Thus our approach is designed to assist in your personal as well as your professional development—in fact, we see the two as inextricably linked. Each of us develops differently as a

teacher because each of us has a different personality, different abilities, different values. We don't want every student who uses this book to come to the same conclusions or to teach the same way. We encourage you to explore yourself and develop your own style and your own identity as a teacher, and we hope to help you to do just that.

We have found that our own students go through three stages in the process of becoming teachers of young children. First, they develop *awareness* of themselves as people and as potential teachers by examining their own values, experiences, and personal qualities. Second, they acquire *knowledge* about child development and early childhood education. And, third, they put what they have learned about themselves and about children into practice and thus gain the basic *skills* they need to work with young children. Each chapter in our book is designed to increase your awareness, to give you information, and to help you develop skills in some area of teaching young children. We have divided each chapter into six parts:

1. *Purpose and Objectives:* To let you know the kinds of awareness, information, and skills discussed in the chapter.

2. *Information:* To give you the information you will need to develop a basic understanding of the subject.

3. *Activities:* To allow you to use that information and thus to develop skills in working with children in classroom settings.

4. *Discussion Guide:* To provide an opportunity to discover the meaning each topic has for you and to share it with other students.

5. *Resources:* To point the way toward further information about each area.

6. *Self-assessment:* To help you evaluate your own learning in terms of the objectives of the chapter. Since professional development is an ongoing process, you may wish to reassess yourself periodically as you gain more understanding and experience.

This book is organized so that each section lays the foundation for the following sections. The organization is graphically represented in the form of a triangle (see page 7). A firm base is essential for strength and durability. The first four chapters form such a foundation, the base of the triangle. In them, we deal with the basic assumptions which shape all our interactions with children. In Chapter 1, "The Teacher," and Chapter 2, "Values," we ask you to look inward at your conception of the role of the teacher, at your own personal characteristics, and at the values you hold for education. In Chapters 3 and 4, we present some of the basic information you will need to understand the development of young children and the many programs designed to teach them. Specifically, we help you, in Chapter 3, "Human Development Theory," to examine the existing body of knowledge about human development and how it relates to teaching, and, in Chapter 4, "History and Models," to examine the past as it relates to work with young children.

The fifth chapter, "Observation," gives you a basic and extremely valuable tool for your work with children. Skill in observation is useful in all areas of teaching. To illustrate this idea in our graphic visualization, we have put *Observation*

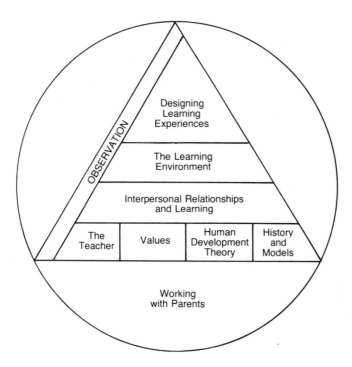

along the left side of the triangle so that it intersects all the levels represented within the triangle itself.

In the next three chapters, "Interpersonal Relationships and Learning," "The Learning Environment," and "Designing Learning Experiences," we describe how you can create and implement a good daily program for young children. Interpersonal Relationships is closest to the base of the triangle because good relationships are absolutely essential in working with young children and helping them to learn. The environment comes next because it provides the structure and raw materials for learning. Learning experiences are at the top of the triangle because they rest upon all of the other areas.

The final chapter, "Working with Parents" examines the teacher's role in helping parents to contribute to the growth and development of their children and introduces ways in which parents can become involved in the early childhood program. We portray working with parents as a surrounding circle because everything we do in programs for young children takes place in the context of sharing and coordinating with parents.

This is not a traditional textbook, nor is it a book of recipes which will tell you the right means to be a teacher of young children. We have designed this book to support your development and we hope that you will find it useful and personally meaningful.

1
The Teacher

PURPOSE AND OBJECTIVES

This chapter is intended to help you, the prospective teacher, to develop an understanding of the nature of the teacher as a person and a professional. In it we will explore the role of the teacher, the nature of teacher authority and the significance of the teacher's personal characteristics. We will also encourage you to become aware of your own personal qualities and how they may influence the ways you will work with young children. Specifically, the objectives for this chapter are that you:

1. Understand the concept of teacher role and some of the major roles played by teachers of young children.
2. Understand the concept of teacher authority and its implications for teaching.
3. Understand how a teacher's personal style may influence the ways in which she interacts with children.
4. Understand the kinds of biases that teachers bring to their job and how these may affect children.

5. Become aware of your own feelings, attitudes, and personal style and the ways these may influence your relationships with children and the choices you will make about teaching.

THE TEACHER

Before looking at the things you will need to know and do in order to teach young children, we want to look at the very nature of teaching and to ask: For what purpose do we intervene in the lives of children?

Recent research in child development has demonstrated that the early years have a significant effect on the child's later development. We know today that young children are learning all the time and from every experience. They are naturally active and curious. They want to make sense of things. Maria Montessori, the famous educator, described the young child as an explorer trying to fit the pieces of a giant puzzle together to make sense out of his world. Because teachers of young children have a great impact on the lives of children, they need to respect children's natural drive for learning and for mastery. And they need to ask themselves when, how, and in what ways it is appropriate for them, as teachers, to intervene in this natural process.

Critics of our educational system have often pointed out that children who enter school lively and inquisitive at three, four, or five years of age often become bored, passive, and even hostile by the time they reach the second or third grade. Schools which emphasize rote learning, unquestioning obedience, and rigid rules and routines may be responsible for such transformations. They view children as vessels to be filled or geese to be stuffed. But when schools are based on what we now know about the growth and development of children, students remain eager and curious, and learning becomes a lively and meaningful process.

Today's developmental early childhood programs come out of a tradition of education which has always emphasized children's natural inclination to grow and learn and which has always regarded teaching as a process of releasing natural potential rather than of providing facts and regimenting behavior. Teaching in a developmental program is like tending a garden: the potential for growth is present in the young sprouts, but they must be carefully tended in order to grow and to flourish. We begin our exploration of the teaching process by focusing on the teacher—the gardener in our image. In this chapter, we will consider the role of the teacher, explore some differences between teachers of young children and other kinds of teachers, and examine the sources of the teacher's authority and the importance of her self-awareness and personal qualities.

Teacher Role

Being a teacher is no small undertaking. Society has many varied and sometimes contradictory expectations about what the role of the teacher should be. In the broadest sense, a role is what a person does because he or she occupies a particular position in an organization or group. When we think of a teacher, we have a general idea that he or she is a person who interacts with students with the purpose of having some kind of learning occur. The kinds of behaviors and strategies which the teacher uses to produce learning vary greatly. Some teachers see their role as communicating information. Others are concerned with helping children learn to live with each other in groups. We are concerned with preparing you to teach in the kind of program we call *developmental*. Developmental programs can vary greatly in the values emphasized, organization, curriculum, and teacher role, but they share a focus on the total development of the child.

The teacher of young children differs from other teachers in that she often plays both the role of the teacher *and* parent. Because preschool and kindergarten children are young, inexperienced, and in a period of transition between home and school, they are more vulnerable and need more nurture and support than older children. The teacher of young children functions, at various times, as a source of warmth and nurture, an organizer of the environment, the provider of resources, and the facilitator of learning. She is, during a single day, a friend, mother, colleague, nurse, and janitor, as well as a teacher. In

short, the teacher of young children is called upon to perform numerous tasks—and not all of them are pleasant. Often our students, who had visions of shaping young minds, are discouraged when they discover how much of their time was spent mopping floors and wiping noses. Working with young children can be—and often is—challenging and rewarding; it can also be tiring and demanding—hard, dirty work.

Because early childhood programs offer a very important transition from the home and deal with children who are not yet fully self-sufficient, the role of the early childhood teacher is larger and more complex than that of other teachers. The teacher must take into account all areas of the child's development.

> *Emotional development.* Helping the child to understand himself and others, to deal with and express feelings, and to develop sensitivity, self-awareness, self-knowledge, and self-esteem.

Social development. Helping the child learn to function in a group of adults and children, and to adjust to the expectations of the school setting.

Intellectual development. Helping the child to acquire information and understanding about the world.

Physical development. Helping the child acquire strength, stamina, coordination, flexibility, and sensory awareness.

Teachers of young children are concerned with all of these aspects of development, although most consider some aspects more important than others. The extent to which a teacher stresses one kind of development over another depends largely on her values and her long-term goals, the kind of program she works in, and all of these will influence the way she designs daily experiences to meet the needs of children. A classroom is a busy and active place and a teacher is called upon to make hundreds of decisions each day. Take, for example, a situation in which two children are struggling for the last ball of clay. The teacher has many choices about how to respond to the children. If she places heavy emphasis on a child's emotional development, she may help the children focus on and discuss their feelings about the situation. If she is concerned with a child's social development, she might help the children examine the problem and seek a joint solution. If the teacher is primarily interested in a child's intellectual or physical development, she might solve the problem as quickly as possible so that the children can go back to working with the clay. Each teacher will have more deeply held priorities in some areas of development than in others, and her priorities may differ from situation to situation.

Teacher Authority

In order to fulfill the requirements of her role, the teacher needs to have authority. *Authority* is defined by Webster as "The power or right to give commands, enforce obedience, take action and make decisions." When we examine the authority of the teacher we find that it comes from a number of different sources. The most obvious source of the authority a teacher has is her adulthood. Because the teacher is larger, stronger, and more knowledgeable than they are, children experience her as being a powerful person. Teachers are, in fact, powerful people in the lives of children, and this carries with it a responsibility for contributing to their growth and development.

Souper (1976) describes four additional sources of the teacher's authority.

1. Simply because she *is* the teacher, she *has* authority.
2. A teacher has a skill or a mastery over a body of knowledge, and this gives her authority.
3. A teacher has a wide experience and a broad understanding, and this gives her authority.
4. A teacher has commitment and other personal qualities, and these too give her authority.

We have watched students and teachers struggle with their notions of authority as they sought to define their relationships with children in ways that felt natural and comfortable to them. Some try to deny the authority that the role of the teacher carries with it. They talk to and treat children as friends and equals. When the children do not treat them with respect, they often become confused and uncomfortable. Others expect children to respect them simply because they are the teacher. They seem to feel that children have to "learn who is boss," have to "accept authority." Often they are surprised by the amount of resistance they encounter from children.

Our students have found George Dennison's concept of "natural authority" very useful:

> Natural authority is a far cry from authority that is merely arbitrary. Its attributes are obvious; adults are larger, are experienced, possess more words, have entered into prior agreements among themselves. When all this takes on a positive instead of merely negative character, the children see adults as protectors and as sources of certitude, approval, novelty, skills [Dennison, 1969, p. 24].

Authority which is authentic and lasting is based on mutual respect and not on coercion. It is used wisely and with compassion.

The rate of growth and learning in children is closely linked to the teacher's personal qualities and her capacity for good relationships with others. In fact, a teacher's sensitivity to young children and her skills in gaining trust and developing relationships are essential first steps in helping them to learn. Such sensitivity and such skills are acquired as teachers come to know themselves and accept themselves. Striving to know herself, the teacher of young children must frequently ask herself, "Who am I?" Major humanistic psychologists—Carl Rogers, Abraham Maslow, and Arthur Jersild—have shown us how valuable it is for us to ask ourselves this question. In order to become what Rogers calls an *authentic* person—one who possesses awareness and empathy, and who is willing to communicate openly with others—we need to *know* ourselves and *accept* ourselves. Out of self-knowledge and self-acceptance, we become what Maslow calls *self-actualized*. A self-actualized person is a person whose actions are an unrestrained, authentic, and creative expression of that person's *self*.

In order to become a caring and nurturing teacher of young children, a person must be able to look at herself as well as others.

Understanding of others can only grow from self-knowledge and self-acceptance, including the ability to be open to new experiences, to acknowledge and deal with the resulting personal feelings, and to experience relationships in ever increasing depth and breadth. This capacity to know and accept oneself is related to the capacity to accept others with caring and without prejudice and to participate in constructive ways in their growth. This is what Jersild is saying when he describes what it is to be compassionate:

> To be compassionate, one must be able to accept the impact of any emotion—love or hate, joy, fear, or grief—tolerate it and harbor it long enough and with sufficient absorption to accept its meaning and to enter into a fellowship of feeling with the one who is moved by the emotion. This is the heroic feature of compassion in its fullest development: to be able to face the ravage of rage, the shattering impact of terror, the tenderest promptings of love, and then to embrace these in a larger context, which involves an acceptance of these feelings and an appreciation of what they mean to the one who experiences them.

The Teacher as a Person

> To be compassionate means to partake in passion: the passions of others, the passions that arise within oneself. It means to participate in feeling rather than simply to view it as a spectator might [Jersild, 1955, pp. 125–26].

Teacher's Feelings

All of us, adults and children, respond to our experiences with strong feelings—joy, rage, envy, frustration, tenderness. As teachers who are also genuine human beings it is important to become aware of the full range of our feelings, express them honestly and constructively and learn to respond with acceptance to children's expression of their feelings.

Teachers sometimes avoid and resist feelings that they do not feel are appropriate. Some teachers feel that they should love all children and that their role calls for them to be sweet and pleasant all the time. These teachers do not realize that even those feelings that society labels as negative are a part of them and can be expressed in ways that do not hurt children or damage their feelings about themselves. When a teacher smiles through clenched teeth at a child who has just made her furious she is being dishonest and both she and the child know it. Similarly, a teacher may resist feelings of love and joy because she doesn't feel comfortable in having or expressing them. But ignoring feelings does not mean that they are not there. And denied feelings tend to show up in disguised forms—as anxiety, guilt, anger. These disguised feelings often have an undesirable impact on children, who are confused about what the teacher is feeling and about how to respond to her.

One of our students, expressing her awareness that she will react strongly to children, wrote:

> There will be many times when my attitudes are not facilitative of learning. I will find myself suspicious of children. I will find it impossible to accept attitudes which differ strongly from my own. I will be unable to understand some of the feelings that are different from my own. I may find myself angry and resentful of children's attitudes towards me, and angry at their behaviors. I may find myself strongly judgmental and evaluative. I want to be able to deal with these aspects of myself as coming from within myself [Chang, 1976].

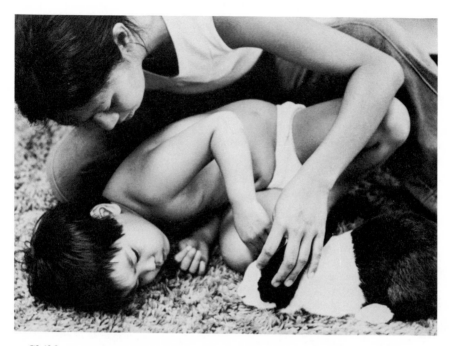

Children express their feelings in passionate ways. Often they express them in ways that do not conform to the rules of our culture. Teachers sometimes react negatively to the ways children express feelings instead of observing and exploring their responses. When, for example, a child says to his teacher, "I hate you, and I wish you would die," the teacher's self-confidence may be shaken. But if she is accustomed to observing and accepting her own reactions, she will be able to accept the child's feelings and to handle them constructively without feeling personally injured and without needing to retaliate.

Teacher's Biases

A teacher brings to her job her whole history and cultural upbringing. Her personal and cultural values color her feelings and influence her responses to individual children, groups of children, and to different kinds of child behavior. As a result of previous experiences, we all tend to have biases—leanings or inclinations to favor or reject certain kinds of people. Sometimes these biases are so strong that we become prejudiced—

form opinions about individuals or groups of people based on our preconceived ideas rather than direct experience.

Teachers are often unaware of their biases and prejudices and the impact these can have on children. To discover something about your own preferences and biases, ask yourself the following questions:

> How do I feel about children who are dirty, ragged, and unattractive, or who fail to conform to my expectations for behavior?
>
> Are there children I immediately dislike or with whom I feel uncomfortable? What are the characteristics of these children?
>
> Do I have strong feelings about loud, aggressive boys or quiet, docile girls?
>
> Do I ignore slow, passive children and focus on lively, verbal ones?
>
> How do I feel in settings when I have to interact with children from unfamiliar ethnic groups?

If you discover that you do have biases, simple awareness may be enough to help you remember, for example, the special needs of a shy child or to remember not to overreact to an aggressive one. Self-observation and the resulting awareness may help you to know when you may be damaging a child by rejecting him or punishing him for things he cannot control. If you become aware that you have prejudices that cannot be overcome, you should look at them as honestly as you can and should ask yourself if there are particular children or groups of children with whom you should not work.

Personal Style

It is important to become aware of your own style and to build upon its strengths. A person whose style is naturally quiet and reserved can be as successful interacting with children as a person whose style is lively and bouncy. Neither style is the best way to relate to children. Both serve equally well.

Your awareness of personal style can help you choose a setting which allows you to function best as a teacher. If, for example, lots of activity, noise, and mess makes you feel anxious and overwhelmed, you might work best in a school which is orderly and quite structured. On the other hand, if you enjoy activity and creative exuberance, you might feel constricted in a highly structured program and prefer working in a more informal one.

Personal Implications

"Who am I?" and "Who am I in the lives of children?" are questions that need to be asked constantly. They remain before each one of us throughout our lives. The answers to these questions become deeper and more meaningful as we gain awareness, understanding, and experience.

We are convinced that the most important characteristic of a good teacher is her ability to be *with* children and not what she does to or for children. Being with children means being really there, aware of the child and yourself in relationship to the child.

As a student in an early childhood education program, you will have opportunities to interact with diverse groups of children in a variety of settings. You may also discover whether you *really* want to be a teacher of young children. A student we know discovered that teaching was not for her when she observed that she was encouraging a child to put on his own shoes and socks, not because she wanted him to become more independent but because she didn't want to get "too close to his smelly little feet." These encounters will provide invaluable opportunities for examining your own feelings and reactions and for discovering your personal style. Your attentiveness to your feelings and reactions will help you become more sensitive to your impact on children, more aware of the types of children and situations which best suit you.

REFERENCES

Chang, Cheryl. Paper for EDCI 316, Early Childhood Education Program, Department of Curriculum and Instruction, University of Hawaii, Honolulu, Hawaii, 1976.

Dennison, George. *The Lives of Children.* New York: Vintage Books, 1969.

Gazda, George M. et al. *Human Relations Development: A Manual for Educators.* Boston: Allyn & Bacon, 1973.

Jersild, Arthur. *When Teachers Face Themselves.* New York: Teacher's College Press, 1955.

Krishnamurti, J. *The First and Last Freedom.* Wheaton, Ill.: Theosophical Publishing House, 1968.

Maslow, Abraham. *Toward a Psychology of Being,* 2nd ed. New York: Van Nostrand Reinhold, 1968.

Rogers, Carl. *Freedom to Learn.* Columbus, Ohio: Charles E. Merrill, 1969.

Seaberg, Dorothy I. *The Four Faces of Teaching: The Role of the Teacher in Humanizing Education.* Pacific Palisades, Calif.: Goodyear Publishing, 1974.

Souper, Patrick. *About to Teach.* London and Boston: Routledge, Kegan and Paul, 1976.

ACTIVITIES

Report on the activities assigned below by:

1. Writing a 3–5 page reaction paper.
2. Using another medium (tape, photography, drawing, etc.) with the instructor's consent.

1. Choose a child for your observation. For at least one hour put yourself in the child's shoes and try to experience the classroom as this child might experience it. Describe as thoughtfully as you can what happened to the child during the period of your observation and how the child might have felt. Focus especially on his interaction with the teacher. What did you learn from this activity about children's feelings, about teachers, and about yourself?

2. Observe a teacher in an early childhood program for at least one hour and describe your impressions of the following:

The professional role the teacher is assuming.

The kind of authority the teacher appears to be exercising.

The qualities of the teacher, including personal style, the ways in which she handles feelings, and the extent to which she appears to be open and genuine.

The teacher's relationship with the children. The implications of this observation for you as a future teacher.

3. Explore your thoughts about yourself as a future teacher of young children in each of the following areas:

What you see as the appropriate professional role of the teacher.

The impact of the teacher's authority and how it should be exercised.

Your personal style, the way you handle your feelings and your ability to be authentic in your relationships with others.

4. If these activities do not challenge you, design your own activity with the consent of the instructor.

DISCUSSION GUIDE

1. In your discussion group share how you remember yourself as a child entering school. What were your feelings about teachers? How did they relate to you and you relate to them?

2. Choose a teacher you remember quite vividly and share your experience in terms of the following issues:
Her role as a teacher.
The source of her authority.
The kind of person she was and the effect this had on the students.
Your perception of the relationship you had with her.

3. Choose a teacher you have observed recently and share your observations concerning her role in terms of the following issues:
Her view of her role as teacher.
Her use of authority.
The relationship of her personal characteristics (self-knowledge, biases, and personal style) to her work with young children.

4. How do you think your personal characteristics (strengths, weaknesses, personal style, etc.) will be likely to affect your work with young children?

5. What kind of relationship would you like to develop with children?

RESOURCES

Almy, Millie. *The Early Childhood Educator at Work.* New York: McGraw-Hill, 1975.

Ashton-Warner, Sylvia. *Teacher.* New York: Simon and Shuster, 1965.

Dennison, George. *The Lives of Children.* New York: Vintage Books, 1969.

Gazda, George M. et al. *Human Relations Development: A Manual for Educators.* Boston, Mass.: Allyn and Bacon, 1973.

Hymes, James. *Teaching the Child Under Six.* Columbus, Ohio: Charles E. Merrill, 1963.

Jersild, Arthur. *When Teachers Face Themselves.* New York: Columbia University Bureau of Publications, 1955.

Katz, Lilian. "Teaching in Preschools: Roles and Goals." *Children,* 17 (March–April 1970): 42–48.

Krishnamurti, J. *Krishnamurti on Education.* New York: Harper and Row, 1974.

Maslow, Abraham. *Toward a Psychology of Being,* 2nd edition. New York: Van Nostrand Reinhold, 1968.

Moustakas, Clark. *The Authentic Teacher,* rev. ed., Cambridge, Mass.: Howard A. Doyle, 1966.

Rogers, Carl. *Freedom to Learn.* Columbus, Ohio: Charles E. Merrill, 1969.

Seaberg, Dorothy I. *The Four Faces of Teaching: The Role of the Teacher in Humanizing Education.* Pacific Palisades, Calif.: Goodyear Publishing, 1974.

SELF-ASSESSMENT

After you have completed the reading, activities, and small-group discussions, look again at the chapter objectives. Write a short paper responding to the following questions.

1. How would you describe your awareness, knowledge, and skill regarding the subject matter of this chapter before you began reading it and doing the activities?

2. To what extent do you feel that you have achieved each of the objectives presented at the beginning of the chapter?

3. What do you see as your strengths in this area?

4. In what specific areas do you need more information and experience? What kinds?

2

Values

PURPOSE AND OBJECTIVES

This chapter is designed to help you, the prospective teacher, to look inward at your values for education and child development. In it we encourage you to explore your values, to examine the importance of congruence between values and actions, and to begin to develop a personal philosophy of teaching based on your values. Specifically, the objectives for this chapter are that you:

1. Become aware of your values for child development and education.
2. Develop skill in observing value choices in yourself and in classrooms you visit.
3. Understand the importance of congruence between a teacher's stated values and actual behavior.
4. Understand the implications of the interaction between program structure and the teacher's personal qualities.

VALUES

"Would you tell me, please,
which way to go from here?"
asked Alice. "That depends a good deal
on where you want to get to," said the cat."
—*Lewis Carroll*
Alice in Wonderland

This quote from *Alice in Wonderland* has important implications for teaching for how can we decide what to do in our classrooms when we do not know where we are going? And decisions about where we are going are, to a great extent, based on values.

In this chapter we will examine the role that values play in the decisions that teachers make about how to guide children's development. We will start our examination by taking a brief look at the nature of values and the way they are chosen.

Much of life is a process of sorting, examining, and acting upon what we value. Values are the beliefs, goals, and attitudes which a person prizes and has chosen on the basis of information and experience. A value stands the test of challenge by others with different beliefs.

Values underlie most of our important life decisions—both personal and professional. Much that goes on in the classroom is a reflection of the teacher's values, and many arguments about education are based on value differences. For example, in colleges and universities disputes often occur between those professors who are primarily concerned with the quality of their teaching and those who are primarily concerned with doing research. Such disputes can become arguments about who is right and who is wrong or they can be acknowledged for what they really are—disagreements based on differences in values. In the field of early childhood education, it is futile to argue what specific educational practices are best without first agreeing on the values a program should reflect. Focusing first on values can help avoid confusion and problems and enhance communication among educators.

Values grow out of our cultural background and upbringing, and out of our individual experiences and preferences. The development of values is a complex process; our values evolve and change as we evolve and change, and value choices often involve conflicting demands—a weighing and balancing.

Although by definition no value or set of values is inherently better or worse than any other, most societies prize those attitudes and actions which support human life and the survival of the species. Teachers in developmental programs for young children value those practices that recognize the humanness and dignity of people and the educational practices that support the development of children's potential while enhancing their sense of self-worth. They also place a high value on the teacher qualities of empathy, self-awareness, respect for children, and openness to experience.

Teachers who rely on the values of others tend to jump from one teaching technique to another without examining whether their actions are consistent or if these really represent what they want for children. But when teachers examine their own values they become more aware of the long-range implications of their decisions. They can weigh their decisions carefully and choose alternatives with clarity and wisdom.

The opportunity to examine values and develop a teaching style and philosophy based on what you value is an essential step in becoming a teacher.

Values and Teaching

Two principal factors contribute to the formation of educational values—the assumptions one makes about people as learners and the views one has about society.

Teachers who feel that the world demands people who are self-directed, caring, creative, and capable of adapting to rapid change tend to believe that people are motivated by an innate desire to learn and grow. Those who hold this view believe in encouraging the growth of the whole child with equal emphasis on all areas of development. They see their role as providing a structured environment rich in resources, in which they help children formulate questions about their experiences and express their ideas.

On the other hand, teachers who feel that people need to conform to the requirements of the society through mastering a body of existing knowledge and skills tend to see people basically as receptive and molded by their environment. Teachers who hold this view act as providers of knowledge and major

sources of wisdom and authority in the lives of children.

Neither of these positions is necessarily best for all children or all teachers. Valuable educational experiences can grow from a variety of viewpoints and have a variety of goals. Good programs for young children can be designed to serve the values of the teacher, the values of the parents and community, *and* the needs of the children. Such programs can reflect many different values and still be based on what is known about child growth and learning.

We have defined the two major value emphases in early childhood programs. We give the term *process-centered* to those educational programs in which learning is an ongoing process of exploring and questioning and in which it is believed that children will choose the activities they need for growth. Advocates of this type of program believe that school experience should be rich and meaningful for children—that education is life, not just preparation for life.

We refer to programs that place major emphasis on the acquisition of specific knowledge and skills as *content-centered*.

In such programs, *what* is learned is more important than *how* it is learned. Advocates of this type of program believe that without controls and structures, time is lost—time in which the child could be gaining important information and skill needed for future success.

As we noted above, neither the process-centered nor content-centered position is necessarily always best. When taken to extreme, either may damage young children. We will refer to programs that provide either too much or too little structure for children's learning as *nondevelopmental*.

There are some programs, often in free schools or alternative schools, which do not provide the necessary structure, stimulation, and interactions that young children need in order to grow and learn. These can be described as *laissez-faire* (hands off programs).

At the other extreme are programs in which mastery of specific tasks is emphasized almost to the exclusion of other developmental goals. Frequently these programs regard the child as a machine to be programmed by systematic reward and punishment. These can be described as *academic* programs.

These extremes can be portrayed on the following continuum:

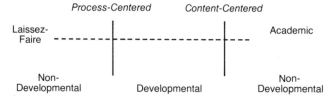

To help teachers examine whether their values for children are consistent with the choices they make in daily practice, we have developed a guide for observing value choices in classrooms called *Dimensions of Educational Structure* (DES) (Figure 1). DES illustrates basic value choices a teacher makes in designing and implementing an educational program (although we designed the DES for use in early childhood pro-

Dimensions of Educational Structure*

---

*Adapted from "Values Examination: A Crucial Issue in Early Childhood Education," in J. D. Andrews (Ed.) *Early Childhood Education: It's an Art? It's a Science?* Washington, D. C.: NAEYC, 1976, pp. 129–36.

PROCESS-CENTERED EDUCATION   CONTENT-CENTERED EDUCATION

Assumptions and Values

People as growth-seeking —————————— People as shaped by the environment
Motivation to learn comes from within the person ——— Motivation to learn based on rewards
Development of the whole person ——————— Development of understanding and skills
Autonomy ——————————————————— Conformity

The Teaching Process

Based on needs and interests of learner ——————— Predetermined curriculum
Use of experience ————————————————— Use of symbols
Learner-initiated ————————————————— Teacher-initiated
Process-oriented ——————————————— Task- or product-oriented
Learner-chosen use of time ————————— Teacher-chosen use of time
Learner-chosen use of space ————————— Teacher-chosen use of space
Learner-chosen use of equipment ——————— Teacher-chosen use of equipment

Figure 1.   Dimensions of Educational Structure.

grams, we have found that it has been useful for helping us examine our college classes as well).

The value choices in the DES include general issues, such as beliefs about human nature, as well as practical program considerations. Each of these choices is presented on a continuum. The two extreme positions on each continuum are given, even though most decisions fall within the extremes.

The DES can be used by the prospective teacher to observe teacher's value choices by checking the point on the continuum which best represents what she observes in a classroom. Our students have used the DES to observe and compare a variety of early childhood programs, and to increase their awareness and sensitivity to the relationship between what they value and what they actually do in their interactions with children. The practicing teacher can use the DES to see if her behavior, classroom organization, and curriculum are really consistent with her values.

Choosing the values that you will act upon is not always a simple process. For example, teachers who are trained in a developmental approach often find themselves caught between their belief that children learn best through the process of play and exploration and pressures from parents who want an academically oriented program in which their children learn to read and write. A teacher who is sensitive to both parent's and children's needs will find this a difficult dilemma and will try to find a solution which will best serve children's development and also communicate her respect for the parents. This may involve giving parents information about the rationale for her viewpoint, accepting the validity of the parents' position for their children, or seeking to find a balance between the two views.

There are also many times when a teacher is faced with the choice between two positive values which conflict with each other—for example, how to support children's spontaneous expression and creativity and the desire to maintain order and tranquillity in the classroom.

It is important for a teacher to be clear on her basic values and educational goals for children and to behave as much as possible in ways consistent with these values. Teachers are sometimes not aware of their basic values or that they state a set of values in direct contradiction to their actual behavior. A teacher may claim to value independence, for example, but organize her classroom so there is never an opportunity for children to work independently or to make choices. Thus, actual behavior goes against the very thing the teacher may wish to accomplish. The teacher should continually evaluate the match between her values and her actual practice in the classroom. Frequently her decisions will not fall consistently on one side of the DES chart or the other. This is to be expected, because each teacher and each situation varies. However, it is useful for the teacher to be aware of how each choice she makes relates to her long-range educational goals for children. When a teacher notices discrepancies between her values and her classroom behavior, she needs to think about whether she wants to change what she does or adjust her values. It is only from a constant evaluation that one's values will become clear and one's approach will become consistent.

Values and Teacher Behavior

Children tend to do what adults *do* regardless of what they say. Consequently, the behavior that the teacher demonstrates in the classroom is very important. Research in classrooms has shown that children learn to be aggressive or cooperative by observing their teachers; that children who observe adults in problem-solving tasks are able to solve problems more readily than those who have not had that experience, and that the level of thinking expressed by the teacher sets the level for student thinking. (Good & Brophy, 1973; Saiwin, 1969). It is apparent from these and other studies that children's behavior will be substantially influenced by the teacher's behavior in the classroom.

The quality of the educational experience you provide as a teacher is greatly influenced by your values. But only when your behavior is consistent with your values do your actions have a positive impact on the lives of children.

It is important to be clear about your values and aware of the extent to which what you say and do in the classroom actually reflects those values. Classroom practice must also rest on the firm base of your knowledge of child development. A teacher who knows how children learn and grow would not, for example, require that young children sit quietly for long periods of

time filling out workbooks. Nor would she allow them to run wild in a messy and disorganized classroom.

Value Choices and Teacher Qualities

The personal characteristics of the teacher appear to be significant in determining the quality and effectiveness of early childhood programs. The extent to which a teacher is authentic—open, self-aware, caring, and genuinely respecting of others—is an essential component of her ability to nurture children and provide for their development.

There is an interaction between a teacher's choices about program structure and her personal qualities. This interaction can be graphically portrayed using four broad classifications in order for us to understand its implications for teaching. A teacher's values can be categorized from the distinctions we made in the DES as primarily process-centered or content-centered (see Figure 2). Teachers can also be put into two

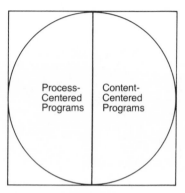

Figure 2.

groups based on whether or not they have the personal quality of authenticity. (see Figure 3). These two figures, when overlaid, create a four-part division. Such a division represents the interaction between value choices and teacher qualities (see Figure 4).

Quadrant I represents the authentic, caring teacher in a process-centered setting. The teacher in a developmental preschool who provides a rich and varied environment and who is deeply concerned with having children learn to deal with their feelings and handle their relationships with peers often fits in this category.

Quadrant II represents the inauthentic teacher in a process-centered school. We have seen this type of teacher in "free" schools and preschools in which the physical setting is not suf-

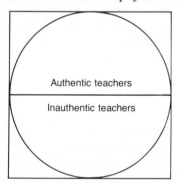

Figure 3.

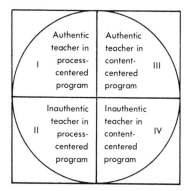

Figure 4.

ficiently structured, in which there is not enough for children to do, and in which teachers appear indifferent or take the role of "one of the kids" instead of providing guidance for relationships and learning.

Quadrant III represents the authentic and caring teacher in a content-centered setting. This type of teacher focuses heavily on curriculum, but she also communicates her fairness, respect, and caring. These teachers are often described with phrases like: "She was really strict and she demanded a lot, but we liked her and I learned a lot that year."

Finally, Quadrant IV represents the inauthentic teacher in a content-centered classroom. This kind of teacher has been vividly portrayed in books about ghetto schools as a rigid tyrant concerned only with having children memorize bits of information that had no relevance to their lives.

Summary

To enhance your own professional development as a teacher who will help young children have rich and meaningful educational experiences in their early years, look inward to discover what you value—the kind of society you want to live in, and what kind of people are needed to make that society work. You then need to examine whether your actions are congruent with what you believe. You ask yourself if what you do in the classroom is based on what is known about how young children learn and grow. You also ask yourself whether you are in touch with your own feelings, and whether you communicate respect and caring to the children.

REFERENCES

Feeney, Stephanie; Phelps, Carol; and Stanfield, Doris. "Values Examination: A Crucial Issue in Early Childhood Education," in J. D. Andrews (Ed.) *Early Childhood Education: It's an Art? It's a Science?* Washington, D. C.: NAEYC, 1976.

Good, Thomas, & Brophy, Jere. *Looking at Classrooms.* New York: Harper and Row, 1973.

Jackson, Phillip. *Life in Classrooms.* New York: Holt, Rinehart and Winston, 1968.

Karpius, Dewayne. "Developing Teacher Competencies," in James Weigand, *Developing Teacher Competencies.* Englewood Cliffs, N.J.: Prentice-Hall, 1971.

Keliher, A. *Talks with Teachers.* Darien, Conn.: Educational Publishing Corp., 1958.

Pickarts, Evelyn, & Fargo, Jean. *Parent Education.* New York: Appleton-Century-Crofts, 1971.

Raths, Louis, & Simon, Sidney. *Values and Teaching.* Columbus, Ohio: Charles E. Merrill, 1966.

Rogers, Carl. *Freedom to Learn.* Columbus, Ohio: Charles E. Merrill, 1969.

Rokeach, Milton. *Beliefs, Attitudes and Values.* San Francisco: Jossey-Bass, 1967.

Saiwin, Enoch. *Evaluation and the Work of the Teacher.* Belmont, Calif.: Wadsworth, 1969.

ACTIVITIES

Report on the activities assigned by:

1. Writing a 3–5 page reaction paper.
2. Using another medium (tape, photography, drawing, etc.) with the instructor's consent.

1. Make a list of at least ten incidents you observe in an early childhood program in which the teacher seems to express a value or make a value choice. What do the incidents suggest about the teacher's values?

2. Rank-order your ten highest values on the accompanying form, "Values I Think Are Important for Children." Would you rank order the same for yourself as you do for children? Are there any others you would include in the list? What experiences in your life do you think contributed to your choice of your top three values? What would teachers and schools need to be like in order to implement these three values? Rank-order from 1 to 24 those qualities that you think are most essential for children to develop as future members of society. Are there any you would add?

3. Choose at least three early childhood programs you have observed and plot them on Figure 1, Dimensions of Educational Structure. Explain why you placed each program where you did on each continuum. Describe your feelings and reactions to each of the programs and how each relates to your own values for education.

4. If these activities do not challenge you, design your own activity with the consent of the instructor.

Values I Think Are Important for Children

Value	Rank Order
1. Happiness	
2. Initiative	
3. A satisfying religious life	
4. Self-respect and self-awareness	
5. Skill, ability and desire to work	
6. True friendship, close companionship	
7. Love of humanity	
8. Fulfillment of individual potential	
9. Use of creative talent	
10. Active participation in democratic process	
11. Responsibility to each other—interdependence	
12. Honest and trustworthy	
13. Cooperation	
14. Freedom, individuality, free choice	
15. Intellectual ability, scholarship	
16. Ability to adjust to and get along in society	
17. A prosperous and successful life	
18. Wisdom	
19. Patriotism	
20. Respect for parents and authority	
21. Social participation	
22. Understanding of ecological needs	
23. Patience and perseverance	
24. Humility	

DISCUSSION GUIDE

1. Using the form "Values I Think Are Important for Children" (p. 46) as the basis for this discussion, share the three values you listed highest. What do you see as the source of these values? What are the implications of these values for you as a future teacher of young children?

2. What kind of world would you like to live in and what would schools have to be like to prepare people to live in that kind of world?

3. What feelings have you had about the early childhood programs you have observed and what can you infer about their values for child development, education, and society?

4. In the early childhood programs you have visited, what activities and practices did you observe that would indicate the child was being encouraged to develop autonomy, creativity, and problem-solving skills? What activities and practices did you observe that suggested that the child was being encouraged to master a predetermined curriculum and conform to adult expectations? .

RESOURCES

Feeney, Stephanie, Phelps, Carol, & Stanfield, Doris. "Values Examination: A Crucial Issue in Early Childhood Education," in J. D. Andrews (Ed.), *Early Childhood Education: It's an Art? It's a Science?* Washington, D.C.: NAEYC, 1976.

Good, Thomas, & Brophy, Jere. *Looking at Classrooms.* New York: Harper and Row, 1973.

Jackson, Phillip. *Life in Classrooms.* New York: Holt, Rinehart and Winston, 1968.

Keliher, A. *Talks with Teachers.* Darien, Conn.: Educational Publishing Corp., 1958.

Moustakas, Clark. *Personal Growth.* Cambridge, Mass.: Howard A. Doyle, 1969.

Pickarts, Evelyn, & Fargo, Jean. *Parent Education.* New York: Appleton-Century-Crofts, 1971.

Raths, Louis, & Simon, Sidney. *Values and Teaching.* Columbus, Ohio: Charles E. Merrill, 1966.

Rogers, Carl. *Freedom to Learn.* Columbus, Ohio: Charles E. Merrill, 1969.

Rokeach, Milton. *Beliefs, Attitudes and Values.* San Francisco: Jossey-Bass, 1967.

SELF-ASSESSMENT

After you have completed the reading, activities, and small-group discussions, look again at the chapter objectives. Write a short paper responding to the following questions.

1. How would you describe your awareness, knowledge, and skill regarding the subject matter of this chapter before you began reading it and doing the activities?

2. To what extent do you feel that you have achieved each of the objectives presented at the beginning of the chapter?

3. What do you see as your strengths in this area?

4. In what specific areas do you need more information and experience? What kinds?

3
Human Development Theory

PURPOSE AND OBJECTIVES

In this chapter we focus on theories of human development and the role of these theories in your understanding of children and your ability to interact with them and contribute to their learning.

In it, we examine the nature of development, the process of formulating theories, and present some theories developed by people who have thought about human development in the past. We then discuss some of the issues that have been generated by differences in their theories. Finally, we turn to the personal and professional implications of your understanding of human development. Specifically, the objectives of this chapter are that you:

1. Understand some basic characteristics of human development.
2. Understand how theory helps you know about and work with children.

3. Understand the nature of four major theories and how knowledge of these affect how we teach children.

4. Become aware of some current issues in the field of human development which have implications for early childhood education.

5. Become aware of some implications of human development theory for working with children.

6. Become aware of some of the developmental factors in your own life and how these may influence you as a teacher of young children.

THEORIES OF DEVELOPMENT

Teachers of young children are often told that it is important that they have an understanding of child development, and they are urged to base educational decisions on such an understanding. But while information about child development can be valuable to the teacher, it is rarely made clear to prospective teachers what information they need or how it can be used in their daily work with children. In this section we want to present basic information about the nature of development and to discuss some of the educational implications which emerge from knowledge of developmental theory.

The Nature of Development

Human development is a process of change in the structure, thought, and behavior of a person. This change results from the interplay of growth, maturation, and experience. Growth is primarily an increase in size. Maturation is an increase in the complexity of organization (both physically and psychologically). Experience is all of a person's interactions with his environment. For example, during the preschool years the body of a child grows—that is, it greatly increases in size and mass. At the same time, maturation is seen in the way the child gradually develops control of his muscles. Such maturation cannot be speeded up through special training. However, it may be retarded by experiences in the environment, such as serious illness or insufficient nutrition.

These same processes of growth, maturation, and experience

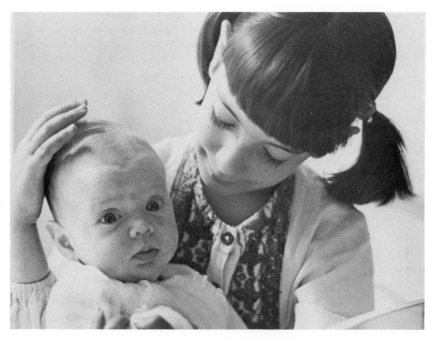

can be seen at work in psychological development as well as in physiological development. For example, an infant lacks the concept of object permanence—that even when an object is not in sight it still exists. No amount of training seems to be able to significantly accelerate the infant's acquisition of this concept (although a lack of experience with objects that are seen, handled, and removed may retard the acquisition).

There are two characteristics common to all human development. First, it proceeds in a direction toward greater size and more complex organization. Second, it proceeds in an orderly, predictable manner. Development takes place through the process of *differentiation* (both physical and psychological) and *integration*. For example, physically, as a fetus grows in the womb, the cells of the body develop different functions; some become muscle tissue, some become specialized organs, some become specialized in other ways. Psychologically, as the child begins to sort out his experiences in the world, he makes differentiations between things that are near to him, such as people who are parents and people who are not. Later, his differentiations reflect greater maturation and experience. He becomes more sophisticated in assigning labels to other things in his environment; for example, moving creatures become specialized to include dogs, cats, cows, giraffes, and elephants. Integration is the process of organizing all these different experiences into managable categories. Eventually the child will organize all the cats, dogs, elephants, etc., in his experience into one inclusive category—animals.

Development is sequential and cumulative since prior levels of size and complexity must precede subsequent ones. Before a child can master the small muscle coordination required to write, for example, he must have had experiences of groping for and grasping objects first, then experiences with paint brushes and scissors, and finally experiences with forming letters with pencils.

The work of Arnold Gesell dealt with the sequential nature of development and the fact that it was dependent on maturation led to the concept of *readiness*—a period of development in which a specific skill or response is most likely to emerge. Readiness can be a useful concept in helping us to have realistic expectations of children but can sometimes lead to passive waiting for the child to get the necessary prerequisite skills rather than providing experiences which will encourage development.

Although the direction and the sequence of development are similar for everyone, each person moves through the process at his own rate and in his own style. Each infant enters the world with his unique biological endowment, and since the interplay of physical, social, and cultural forces are different for every person, it is clear that no two children—even from the same family—are exactly alike.

Developmental Theory

Human beings are naturally curious. They try to organize and make sense out of their experiences of the world. One way to organize experience into comprehensible and useful form is to create a theory. A *theory* is an idea, a plan, or a formulation about the underlying principles of certain observed phenomena that has been verified to some degree. A theory may be thought of as a statement of the relationship among facts. A theory gives us a mental picture of how things are. In the broadest

sense, theory helps us to organize information about the world so that it can be comprehended and acted on.

We construct theories about things that are interesting or important to us by generating hypotheses (educated guesses). *Hypotheses* are tentative explanations which can then be explored and tested by observation and experimentation. When a hypothesis is proven to be true in a number of situations, it becomes a theory. Theories allow us to generalize—to relate, for example, the things we have discovered about one group of people or situations to other similar groups of people or situations.

A teacher uses the theories created by others to give her a base of knowledge about children, and she continually develops, tests, and modifies her own hypotheses about the children she works with.

The theories that educators draw upon to learn about young children were developed, in large part, by experimental psychologists and focus heavily on the areas of motivation and learning. Early childhood educators today are becoming more aware of contributions from other disciplines as well. The fields of biology, genetics, and nutrition contribute valuable information regarding physical development; and social sciences like anthropology and sociology give insight into the impact of social and cultural forces on the developing child.

Each theory provides a lens for viewing development. Yet, we need to be aware that the nature of a theory is profoundly influenced by the basic assumptions of the person or group that creates the theory, for one's point of view influences what one chooses to study and how it is studied.

Theories are constantly being revised. Arthur Combs points out that while theories aid us in understanding of the world, they do not represent truth, which is static and unchanging:

> There are almost unlimited ways in which facts can be organized and each of these may be quite useful and acceptable for understanding a specific thing at a specific time . . . Sooner or later even the best of theories is likely to be superceded by something a little better, simpler, more accurate, more comprehensive, or more useful for accomplishing our purposes [Combs, 1976, p. 11, 13].

Theory is useful for understanding and organizing thought and action. It also has limitations. Theories are often contradictory. They can also be constricting. The adherence to a particular theory can make us inflexible and lead to bias in our thinking. We need to keep in mind that there is no right way to view children and no single theory which ties up everything we need to know about children into one neat package.

Developmental Theories and Theorists

In this section we discuss four theories which represent major positions found in human development today and the theorists who have articulated them. These include:

- Psychoanalytic Theory: Freud, Adler, and Erikson
- Behaviorist Theory: Skinner
- Cognitive Development Theory: Piaget
- Humanistic Theory: Rogers and Maslow

These theories differ in their underlying assumptions, the

areas of development they focus on, and the subjects and methodology used in their experiments and studies.

No single one of these theories gives a total picture of the development of a person. The situation is like that in the famous story of the blind men and the elephant. "The one who has the trunk says, 'It is long and soft and emits air.' Another holding the legs, says, 'It is massive, cylindrical and hard.' Another touching the skin, 'It is rough and scaly'" (Ornstein, 1972, p. 9). Each man has one part of the picture and each generalizes from particular knowledge.

As in the story of the blind men and the elephant, when we look carefully at theories of development, we may find contradictions among the various viewpoints. Each theory gives us part of the whole. In order to achieve the most complete and accurate understanding of the child, it is useful to combine aspects of various theories to get an ever fuller picture.

Psychoanalytic Theory: Freud and Erikson

Many of the ideas and concepts used today to describe children's social and emotional development derive from the work of Sigmund Freud and his followers. Freud developed a therapeutic technique called *psychoanalysis* as a method of treating neurotic adults. As a result of observations of his troubled patients, Freud came to believe that people were instinctively sexual and aggressive and that a person's psychological disturbances were the result of early life experiences. His assumptions about the basic nature of humans and the process of personality development led him to formulate and articulate a theory that explained what he had observed.

Freud's theory identified the instinctive aspect of humans as the *id*. The id consists of both positive and negative forces—the drive to live, create, and love as well as the capacity to destroy. This highly instinctual aspect of the personality is believed by psychoanalysts to be tempered by the *ego*. The ego is the aspect of the person that keeps the id from wreaking havoc in the world. It is the mediator that keeps reign over the expression of the destructive or unrealistic manifestations of the id. The superego or conscience develops both from expressions of disapproval and threat of censure and from social approval by significant adults.

Freud believed that during the first five years of life, a person passes through a sequence of psychosexual stages of development that greatly influence the course of future development. He identified three stages which occur in these early years, each of which focuses on a different area of the body. Infancy is the *oral stage* in which attention is focused on the mouth. Freud theorized that the quality of feeding experiences tended to contribute to a person's sense of security and his trust of people. The *anal stage* follows, during which the child's development is heavily influenced by toilet experiences. During this stage, Freud believed that any parental actions that caused the child to feel anxious and/or guilty about his ability to control his elimination might lead to the development of excessive personality characteristics, such as perfectionism or stinginess. The *phallic stage,* between ages three and five, is the period during which the child focuses on his genitals. Freud believed that it was during this stage that the child assumes the proper sexual identity as male or female and that the proper identification is dependent on a meaningful model of the same sex.

Freud introduced the very important concept that behavior is influenced by unconscious factors, many of which originate in the early experiences of the psychosexual stages outlined above, and which are lost to conscious memory through the mechanism of repression.

The psychoanalytic tradition is often criticized because it evolved from the study of neurotic and psychotic people. Many critics believe that it overemphasizes the aggressive, vicious, and unconscious aspects of humans. They also believe that the focus on deficiencies in personality has led to an excessive concern with the development of treatment for the ills, where time could have better been spent on exploring what supports development of a healthy personality.

Freud's theory served as the basis for a number of other theoretical approaches. One approach that has had an influence on early childhood education is the *individual psychology* of Alfred Adler, originally a follower of Freud, who later formed his own psychological theory. Adler's theory assumed that humans were primarily motivated by social urges and that normal development led to the awakening of social responsibility. Late in his life Adler established child guidance clinics in conjunction with Viennese Schools. Today his theory is used as the basis for those child guidance and classroom management programs that emphasize individual responsibility.

Freud's ideas have been revised and expanded by a number of his followers, including his daughter Anna Freud, and Erik Erikson. Freud's followers have worked with children as well as adults and have been interested in identifying conditions which foster healthy social and emotional development.

Erikson has identified a series of stages of social and emotional development which expand the psychosexual stages described by Freud to include social influences. Erikson believes that basic attitudes are formed as individuals pass through stages of social-emotional development and that serious trouble at any stage will lead to difficulty in reaching the next stage. He believes that the home and school can provide understanding, encouragement, and models of behavior that help the child deal successfully with various challenges and to pass to the next stage. For each stage, Erikson describes the potential for healthy development at one end of a continuum, and the potential for development of negative and self-defeating attitudes at the other end. Each stage is characterized by a major task or challenge. In infancy, the major task facing the child is the development of basic trust; for the toddler, it is the development of autonomy; for the preschooler, it is the development of initiative; and for the school-age child, it is the development of industriousness. Although the first and most significant encounter with each of these tasks is made during its crucial period of development, every person needs continuing experiences which contribute to his sense of trust, autonomy, initiative, and industry. In Erikson's work, development is seen as a product of the tension between the two extremes. In order for the child to develop in healthy and positive ways, it is necessary that more experiences be positive than negative.

Following are brief descriptions of the psychosocial stages of the early childhood years derived from Erikson's classic work *Childhood and Society* (1950) in which he outlines the developmental tensions that must be resolved.

Stages of Psychosocial Development:
Erikson

Trust vs. Mistrust (Infancy). During the first stage of life the infant learns or fails to learn that other people can be depended on and that he can depend on himself to elicit nurturing responses from others. The quality of care the infant receives, especially in the first year of his life, is essential to the development of basic trust. Through the love and acceptance he receives, the infant learns that the world is a good and safe place. If he is fed, nurtured, and allowed to move his body according to his own patterns of need, he will develop the foundation for trust.

Autonomy vs. Shame and Doubt (Toddler). During the second stage of life, which begins at 12–15 months, the child develops a basic sense of autonomy—self-control and independent action. During this period the child is growing rapidly. He is learning to coordinate many new patterns of action and to assert himself as a human being. Conflict during this period centers on toilet training. The child learns to hold in and to let go. If parents are accepting and easy-going, and if they recognize the child's developing need to assert his independence, the child will move successfully through this stage. If adults are harsh and punitive, and if the child is punished for assertive behavior, then doubt and shame may become stronger forces in the child's life than autonomy. It is important during this period that the child has opportunities to do things for himself.

Initiative vs. Guilt (Preschool Years). This is a period of interest, active exploration, and readiness for learning. The child needs to express his natural curiosity and creativity during this stage through opportunities to act on his environment. If his explorations are regarded as naughtiness, and if parents or teachers are overly concerned with the child's getting dirty or destroying things, the child may not develop his sense of initiative and guilt may be the more prevalent attitude.

Industry vs. Inferiority (School Age). During this period the child is ready for the challenge of new and exciting ideas and of constructing things. He needs opportunities for accomplishment, both physical, intellectual, and social. He needs many

and varied interaction with materials. Success and the feeling "I can do it!" result in a sense of industry.

Psychoanalytic theory has contributed many important insights into the development of a person that have implications for the teacher of young children. The development of the child was seen by Freudians as progressing through a series of stages that were predictable, continuous throughout life, and influenced by numerous forces that came to bear on the individual. The theory emphasized the importance of the early years in determining later social and emotional development. Because crucial aspects of a child's development occur early in life when the child is very dependent on adults, the relationships between children and their significant adults is highlighted. As teachers, it is important to realize that what you do either for or to children has an impact on their subsequent development. You can influence, negatively or positively, the young child's attitude about himself. When you understand that what you do as a teacher may be vital and irreversible in terms of the development of another human being, you will probably think more about the choices you make in your interactions with children.

Psychoanalytic theory has influenced educational programs by its emphasis on the importance of social and emotional development. By calling attention to the unconscious forces that influence behavior, educators have become aware that children cannot consciously control all of their behavior and are therefore less harsh in their judgments and expectations of young children. It has also made educators more watchful of the personal characteristics of the adults who play the role of teacher in the lives of children.

Behaviorist Theory: Skinner

Behaviorist theory is derived from the work of B. F. Skinner and his predecessors Thorndike, Watson, and Hull. These theorists focus their attention on the role of the environment in shaping behavior.

The primary focus of behaviorist theory is on learning. Learning is viewed as something which involves a change in behavior which can be observed and measured. A great deal of the basic research for the development of behaviorist theory was conducted in carefully controlled laboratory research with animals. The theories have also been tested on human beings with many similar results. Behaviorist theory emphasizes the action of the environment on the individual; external stimulation is seen as the source of growth and change. Langer describes it as a "mechanical mirror" theory:

> Like a mirror, the child comes to reflect his environment; like an empty slate, he is written upon by external stimuli; like a wax tablet, he stores the impressions left by these stimuli; and like a machine, he may be made to react in response to stimulating agents [Langer, 1970, p. 51].

Behaviorists regard the drive to satisfy physical needs as the fundamental force underlying human behavior. Drives spur the individual to activity for as long as the drive remains unsatisfied. Initial activity in response to a drive may be more or less random. But when a behavior aids an individual in achieving satisfaction, that behavior tends to be repeated when the drive is felt again. Learning, according to this theory, consists of the build-up of associations between drives (the stimulus) and the behavior (response) which results in the satiation of the drive. Past associations are stored and will influence responses to new stimulation. According to this view, all that is required to predict behavior and to shape it is a knowledge of past responses and present conditions of stimulation. Because of the important role of stimuli, responses, and the build-up of associations between the two, this theory is often referred to as stimulus-response (S–R) theory.

Behaviorists do not deal with concepts like thought or emotion because they are not observable. The mind is viewed as a mysterious black box whose nature can be inferred only from its actions (Baldwin, 1967, p. 392).

Behaviorist theory differs from other theories of human development in that it is not developmental—it does not see development as progressing through a series of stages. Rather, the same mechanism of learning operates independently of the maturity of the learner.

The implications for education have to do with the effects rewards and punishments have on shaping learning and behavior. Children's behaviors tend to have positive or negative reinforcing consequences. If a behavior is rewarded, it is likely to be repeated; if ignored or punished, the likelihood of its being repeated is less. After a behavior is reinforced a number of times, it will be controlled by the reinforcement. For example, the first time the child puts on his own shoes, he may be imitating a behavior he has seen in others. If this behavior is followed by praise, an enthusiastic hug, or a cookie, it is likely to be repeated.

Many programs for young children focusing on both academic content and behavior management have been developed in recent years using methods derived from behaviorist theory. Behaviorist programs are designed so that the adult defines the goals and shapes the child's behavior. It can be very useful and comforting for a teacher to know that learning can be prescribed by observing a child, determining what she wants him to learn, and discovering a stimulus that will produce the desired response.

On the other hand, early childhood educators are often uncomfortable with the mechanistic implications of applying behaviorist principles in programs for young children.

The use of external rewards such as grades, candy, tokens, and praise may result in children doing activities for approval or for tangible rewards rather than for the inherent pleasure in learning. Behaviorist principles and techniques *do* work. The fact is, reinforced behaviors are most likely to reoccur, whether the rewards are in the form of praise or material objects.

Reinforcement principles are being applied in classrooms all the time, either consciously or unconsciously. It is important that as a teacher of young children you learn to differentiate between what is being reinforced and how, so you can take care to influence behavior in a manner that fits your goals for children. With attention and careful thought, behaviorist principles can be applied in the service of developmental goals.

Cognitive Development Theory: Piaget

Jean Piaget has devoted many years of his life to a systematic, in-depth study of children's thinking. He began his career as a biologist and studied how organisms adapt to their environments. This fascination with biological adaptation evolved into an interest in how people adapt to their environment. Since man's adaptation is largely a function of his ability to use reason, Piaget became interested in the development of the capacity for thought. Piaget's theory focuses primarily on the nature and development of cognition. As Ginsburg and Opper summarize it:

> Piaget is interested in mental activity, in what the individual *does* in his interaction with the world. Piaget believes that knowledge is not given to a passive observer; rather knowledge of reality must be discovered and constructed by the activity of the child [Ginsburg and Opper, 1969, p. 14].

Cognitive developmental theory, based on Piaget's work, stresses adaptation as a result of the transaction between the individual and his social and physical environment. In this theory, the child is seen not as an organism shaped by the environment but as an active agent who causes his own development through his capacity to adapt.

Through careful observation of children, Piaget identified processes and stages of intellectual development. Based on his interaction with the environment, the child develops organizing structures in the mind that Piaget refers to as *schemes.* Initial schemes become the basis for more complex future mental structures.

Adaptation Processes

Piaget identifies three complementary processes that the child employs to organize his experience into structures for thinking and problem solving. The first process is *assimilation,* by which new information or experiences are incorporated into existing mental structures. For example, the child who sees a goat for the first time and calls it a dog is trying to assimilate, that is, use a structure he already has. The second process is *accommodation,* the changing of existing structures to fit external reality more accurately and the creation of new structures. The child has accommodated when he acquires the new structure or scheme—goat. The third process, called *equilibration,* is based on the tendency of the individual to bring about a dynamic balance between the influx of new information and experience and his ability to fit it into existing structures.

Adaptation, the ability to use knowledge, comes about through the interplay of assimilation and accommodation. Piaget defines intelligence as the ability to maintain a balance between these processes.

Piaget's Stages of Cognitive Development

Through the dynamic processes outlined above, the child progresses through a series of developmental stages that build from the interaction between existing mental structures, maturation, and experience. Stages flow into each other in the same sequence for everyone although the exact age at which a child enters the next stage varies with the individual and the culture.

There are two important developmental tasks that represent shifts in the child's development and signal progress into the next stage. The first of these is called *object permanence* and is a major task of infancy. During this stage, the child learns that objects exist in the world apart from his relationship to them—that an object may still exist even after it is out of his sight. The second major task of early childhood is for the child to learn to conserve—to realize that the amount or quantity of a substance stays the same even when its shape or location changes.

Following is a capsule summary of Piaget's stages of cognitive development.

Sensorimotor Period. During this period, from birth to approximately two years of age, the child changes from a reflex organism to one capable of thought and language. Behavior is primarily motor. The child is dependent on physical manipulation until about age two when he begins to be able to form mental images. The infant learns to differentiate himself from objects, seeks stimulation, and begins to develop the concept of object permanence.

Preoperational Period. This period, which spans the ages between two and eight, is characterized by the development of language and rapid conceptual development. The child develops labels for experience, develops the ability to use symbols, and makes judgments according to how a thing looks to him.

The early phase of this period is called *preconceptual*. Between the ages of two and four the child is egocentric, in that he is unable to take the viewpoint of others. He tends to classify by single salient features.

The *intuitive* phase, between four and seven years, finds the child capable of more complex thought, able to elaborate more, and capable of social interaction because of a decrease in egocentrism. It is during this phase that the child gradually develops a concept of *conservation*. Both of these phases are referred to as preoperational because the child is not yet capable of logical thought.

Concrete Operations Period. During this period, between ages seven and eleven, the child develops the ability to apply logical thought to concrete problems. The formal thought processes become more stable and reasonable even though the child still has to think things out in advance and try them in the real world.

Formal Operations Period. Between the ages of eleven and fifteen, the child's cognitive structures reach their greatest level of development as he becomes able to apply logic to all classes of problems. The child develops basic principles of cause and effect and of scientific experimentation. He can weigh a situation mentally to deduce relationships without having to try it out.

Piaget's stages of intellectual development represent major changes in educators' ideas about the nature of children's thinking.

One of Piaget's most important contributions has been to make teachers aware that children's thinking is fundamentally different from the thinking of adults and that the development of adult logic evolves from a series of stages in children's thought. Piaget has described children's thinking as *egocentric,* that is, the child makes conclusions based on how things look to him and not by using adult logic. This is illustrated in the following anecdote. A child on his first plane ride turned to his mother after the plane had completed its ascent

and asked, with great earnestness, "When do we start getting smaller?"

When teachers understand the egocentric nature of children's thought, they respond with understanding and appreciation to their attempts to organize their experience, instead of with condescending humor or ridicule when the child makes the mistake of calling a *giraffe* a *horse* or thinking another child has more because his graham cracker broke into pieces.

Because the child's thinking grows out of his direct experience and action, educators who use Piaget's theory design programs which allow for exploration, experimentation, and many opportunities for direct interaction with materials. The experiences the child has in such programs lay the foundation for the development of his ability to think abstractly later. Piaget is adamant in his insistence that we cannot *teach* children the information they need to progress to the next stage. He has also been critical of the American tendency to want to hurry development rather than to let it follow its own course. What we as caring and sensitive teachers can do is to make available the raw materials the child will need when he is ready for the next step.

Humanistic Theory: Rogers and Maslow

The humanistic view of development was created by psychologists who saw existing theories as inadequate in explaining the nature of human potential. They felt that these theories did not take into account what they saw as the unique qualities of human beings—the capacity for consciousness, for love, and for the desire to illuminate the unknown. Theorists who have formulated a view of development which takes human potential into account came primarily from the relatively new field of humanistic psychology. They are often referred to as *humanists, self-psychologists, phenomenologists, existential* and *perceptual psychologists*. Theorists who have influenced this school of thought include Gordon Allport, Arthur Combs, Carl Rogers, Abraham Maslow, and Rollo May.

Human potential theories have healthy people as their subjects of study and their concern is how to support positive development rather than overcoming neurosis or defining normality. Sources of data include self-observation and observation of people who seem to have reached a high expression of human potential. These examples of the potential of human development are what Maslow refers to as "self-actualized" people. The personal qualities of these people have been identified and serve as a model of what people are capable of becoming.

The focus in humanistic psychology is on understanding behavior from the point of view of the person who is behaving. This means that the feelings, thoughts, and values of the individual are as important as observable behavior in the attempt to make sense of human life. From what the person says and what he does, one can make inferences about his inner life.

The major feature of human potential theory is that it attempts to describe and validate human characteristics that other theories have regarded as too elusive to be the subject of scientific study. These are the very characteristics that constitute humanness: thought, feeling, consciousness, choice, and the capacity to find personal meaning in experience.

Another important characteristic of this theory is seeing the person as an integrated whole whose development takes place in a complex network of interactions with the physical world, the social world, and the world of the unknown.

Finally, human potential theory concerns itself with the quality of human life. It focuses on the affirmation of human dignity and offers a vision of what people are capable of becoming.

Humanistic theory influences the kinds of educational programs educators create for young children by focusing on the development of the whole child, on what the child can become. The focus is on the process of actualizing the individual's potential in all areas—intellectual, social, emotional, artistic, spiritual, and physical.

Humanistic theory has influenced the development of a number of programs which focus on affective (emotional) development—an area which these theorists feel has been neglected in traditional curriculum.

Another implication of humanistic theory has to do with the roles of the teacher and the learner. When the teacher accepts that every person has the potential for finding meaning in the world, for self-awareness and awareness of others, and for making wise choices, then her job becomes one of facilitator or helper, and the child is given maximum opportunity to direct his own learning.

Daniel Jordan and his associates at the University of Massachusetts have formulated an educational model (ANISA) which has a human potential orientation (although it also includes insights from other theoretical perspectives). Jordan has worked to identify the forces that contribute to the greatest possible actualization of human potential. The ANISA model is a valuable first step in organizing existing human development information into a comprehensive theory for teaching young children.

Issues in Developmental Theory

Differences in the various theoretical approaches have generated some basic issues which are still being dealt with in the field of human development. Current efforts to resolve these issues are the basis for most of the ongoing theoretical disputes and the questions being addressed in the field today. The way people respond to these issues has important implications for teaching young children.

Biological vs. Environmental Forces in Development

Biological forces in human development (sometimes referred to as *nature*) take the form of genetic endowment and are manifested through the process of maturation or growth. Environmental forces (sometimes referred to as *nurture*) have to do with the kinds of interactions and experiences which enhance or restrict the development of the child's biological potential. In the past, there was a raging debate—sometimes called the "nature-nurture controversy"—between theorists who felt that biological endowment was the major factor in determining the course of development and those who felt that environment was the most important.

Today, researchers still debate the relative importance of biological and environmental influences on human development, but there is general agreement that heredity and environment interact in complex ways.

Human development specialists are now concerned with providing optimal conditions for development from before conception through the early years. They are interested in prenatal conditions including the health and nutrition of the parents, birth procedures which are less traumatic for mother and child than traditional hospital delivery, and the quality of the environment and nurture provided the infant and young child.

The Significance of the Early Years

Many of our old ideas about human development have become outdated in the light of research done in the last decades. In *Intelligence and Experience,* J. McVicker Hunt describes some of the major changes that have taken place in the way we view child development. Until the 1950s and '60s, our basic belief about children was that intelligence and adult characteristics were predetermined by genetic endowment. Individuals would develop in predictable ways as they matured. A more recent belief is that adult development is influenced by the interaction of various forces and can be greatly modified by early experiences. Studies conducted by Benjamin Bloom (1964), for example, indicated that fifty percent of the characteristics associated with mature intelligence are typically developed by the age of four and that approximately eighty percent are developed by the age of eight. Bloom's work led to the belief that the early years have a very important impact on later social and emotional development. The years between four and eight, in fact, are the most significant time in determining the future course of a person's development.

The belief that inadequate nurturing and stimulation during early development is likely to cause irreversible deficiencies later on was supported by the work of many human development researchers.

Recent work by Jerome Kagan suggests that the early years may not be quite so important as previously thought. Kagan observed and tested a group of Guatemalan Indian children in a remote community who were deprived, during the first two years, of the light of day, had limited interaction with people and play objects, and were fed a limited diet. These children did, however, have physical contact and the loving care of their mothers. Tests done with these children indicated serious lags in development during infancy and early childhood, but at the age of eleven, children from the same village were tested and observed to be functioning normally in all aspects of development. Subsequent explorations by Kagan have uncovered evidence in other regions of the world of normal development following what would be seen by Americans as a very deprived infancy and early childhood.

Kagan's findings do not necessarily dispute the developmental significance of infancy and early childhood, but they do call into question the previous belief that the effect of early deprivation was irreversible.

The controversy about the effects of early experience may be resolved in the future as theorists and researchers continue to explore the relationship between maturation and experience in development.

Continuity vs. Discontinuity in Development

Human development researchers and theorists debate whether change in the structure, thought, and behavior of a developing person are the result of sudden or gradual change. Gradual change is referred to as *continuous development,* whereas sudden change is labelled *discontinuous development.*

Discontinuous development is linked to the concept of stages in which change is seen as occurring in relatively discrete steps that are dependent on changes in physiological structure and requisite developmental experiences.

Theorists who see development as continuous argue that stage theorists tend to identify abrupt and dramatic transitions between ways of thinking and behaving only because of their inability to detect the continuities. Another argument for continuous development is that the interdependence between areas of development is too complex and too interconnected to be explained or triggered simply by a change in physiological structure.

Generally, theorists agree that there may be both continuities and discontinuities in development.

Intrinsic vs. Extrinsic Motivation

A major debate that continues among theorists and researchers in human behavior, and one which has major implications for education, has to do with the nature of motivation. A *motive* is a drive, an incentive, a goal or an intention that causes a person to do something or act in a certain way.

According to behaviorist theory, motivation is extrinsic. Behaviorists believe that organisms are active only when motivated by need which they strive to satisfy in order to return to a state of equilibrium. The motivation to learn is viewed as coming from an expectation of reward.

In the last thirty years, there have been a series of studies which challenged this view of motivation and which suggest that in the absence of need, individuals are naturally curious and will seek stimulation by acting on their environment. J. McVicker Hunt has postulated that there is motivation inherent in spontaneous activity, and Robert White (1959) has referred to this tendency toward exploration and activity as *competence motivation*—a need to bring about an effect through acting on the environment. Spontaneous activity typically takes place when there is freedom from need and a novel kind of stimulation in the environment. Children's play is an example of this kind of spontaneous activity. This view of motivation as intrinsic suggests that people are naturally motivated to be active and curious and that learning is inherently satisfying when there is the right kind of stimulation available.

Implications of Theory for Working with Children

If as a teacher, you recognize that a child is constantly striving to realize his own potential—to gain control over his own body and to organize his experiences in meaningful ways—you will be more likely to see your role as that of a guide who assists the child to accomplish what he is predisposed to do, rather than a director who is responsible for determining the course of the child's development.

The teacher's view of motivation also has far reaching implications for educational practice. If she believes that learning only occurs when rewards are offered, she will build her educational approach on tokens, candy, praise, or grades. If she believes children are intrinsically motivated to make sense out of the world, she will create learning experiences that stimulate their natural curiosity.

Both forms of motivation work. The kind of motivation that the child responds to seems to depend on his previous experience. A child who is allowed to find an inner satisfaction in some activity may tend to feel that that is reward enough. A child who is given external reinforcements for what he does may become accustomed to looking outside himself for approval and reward.

The knowledge that growth is a process which generally follows a definite sequential order in all human beings helps teachers to see and respond appropriately to children in a particular stage of development. Knowledge about each stage lets you know in a general way what can be expected of a child and enables you to plan experiences and hold expectations that are appropriate.

An awareness of the cumulative nature of development helps the teacher recognize that a child cannot be expected to have a kind of awareness, understanding, or skill that his level of development has not prepared him to have. If, for example, a child lacks sufficient maturity and experience, he is simply unable to master the skill of walking. A child who has not gained an awareness of numbers cannot be expected to add or subtract. New experiences that do not build from previous experiences can overwhelm or frighten a child, while an experience which is too much like a previous experience may not be stimulating to the child. J. McVicker Hunt (1971) describes the concept of an *optimal match* between the child's present level of understanding and his acquisition of new information. New experiences need to provide just the right amount of novelty to interest the child and to increase his understanding of something. Teachers can stimulate children's development by providing experiences which challenge them to reach for the next stage of development and by avoiding the introduction of experiences which are frustrating or boring.

Although the sequence of development may be the same for everyone, each person is unique. Each moves through the sequence and develops at his own rate and in his own style. The fact that every child is different from all other children has important implications for teachers who need to respond to each child in terms of his uniqueness and to adjust their expectations accordingly. A teacher who knows stages of development only may make the mistake of believing that every child at a particular stage of development can be expected to behave like all other children at that stage. This viewpoint can lead to teachers who expect all children of a particular age to master the same skill (for example, expecting all six-year-olds to learn to read), rather than adjusting curriculum and expectations to individual needs. The point is, there is a wide range of variation in normal development, and an informed teacher will be aware that the rigid comparison of a child to an arbitrary standard overlooks the fact that each individual has his own unique pattern of development.

A sensitive teacher is aware of the wide range of developmental differences and is also able to detect a child whose variation from developmental norms is so great that it is cause for concern. When she observes such a variation, she needs to watch the child closely, seeking to understand what the problem might be. She may even need to consult a specialist who can make a diagnosis and design a plan for working with the child.

Personal Implications of Developmental Theory

Another way of looking at human development theory is to recognize that you too are in the process of development and are, to some extent, the product of the environmental forces which have shaped you since infancy and which continue to shape you. Your attitudes toward children, social and cultural differences, sex roles, family structures, and acceptable behaviors, are all influenced by the forces which have affected your development. Even the theories you believe in and which guide your actions in working with children are influenced by your own process of development. An awareness of these influences enables you to look at your own responses to children and to discover whether you are providing support for their growth and development.

While theory is a useful tool for organizing information and directing behavior, it provides no ready answers because it has so many limitations. Existing theories of development may be fragmented, contradictory, or possibly biased by the viewpoint of the theorist. So what is the teacher to do when trying to make sense out of masses of information about child development? And if theory does not provide all of the answers, what does the teacher use as a basis for her decision making?

At this point you need to go back to the value questions raised in Chapter 2 and look again at your values for society and education, using them as a basis for examining existing theories in order to choose information that will help you accomplish your long-range goals for children. You, the teacher, are ultimately left with the task of creating your own personal theory, based on your values and your knowledge of children, and your experiences with them.

REFERENCES

Baldwin, A. L. *Theories of Child Development.* New York: John Wiley & Sons, 1967.

Biber, Barbara. "A Learning–Teaching Paradigm Integrating Intellectual and Affective Processes" in *Behavioral Science Frontiers in Education.* Edited by Eli M. Bower and William G Hollister. New York: John Wiley & Sons, 1967.

Biber, Barbara, & Franklin, Margery B. "The Relevance of Developmental and Psychodynamic Concepts to the Education of the Preschool Child." *Journal of the American Academy of Child Psychiatry,* January 1967, 6(1).

Bloom, Benjamin J. *Stability and Change in Human Characteristics.* New York: John Wiley & Sons, 1964.

Brophy, Jere E. *Child Development and Socialization.* Chicago: Science Research Associates, 1977.

Chilton Pearce, Joseph. *Magical Child.* New York: E. P. Dutton, 1977.

Combs, Arthur W.; Richards, Anne Cohen; & Richards, Fred. *Perceptual Psychology.* New York: Harper and Row, 1976.

Cowles, Millie. "Four Views of Learning and Development." *Educational Leadership,* May 1971, 28(8), 790–795.

De Vries, Rheta. "Theory in Educational Practice." In *Preschool Education. A Handbook for the Training of Early Childhood Educators,* edited by Ralph W. Colvin and Esther M. Zaffiro. New York: Springer Publishing Co., 1974.

Elkind, David. *A Sympathetic Understanding of the Child: Birth to Sixteen.* Boston: Allyn and Bacon, 1974.

Erikson, Erik. *Childhood and Society.* New York: Norton, 1950.

Evans, Ellis. *Contemporary Influences in Early Childhood Education.* New York: Holt, Rinehart and Winston, 1970.

Flavell, John H. *Cognitive Development.* New Jersey: Prentice-Hall, 1977.

Frost, Joe L., and Kissinger, Joan B. *The Young Child and the Educative Process*. New York: Holt, Rinehart, and Winston, 1976.

Ginsburg, Herbert, and Opper, Sylvia. *Piaget's Theory of Intellectual Development*. Englewood Cliffs, New Jersey. Prentice-Hall, 1969.

Gordon, Ira J. *Human Development from Birth through Adolescence* (2nd ed). New York: Harper and Row, 1969.

Hamachek, Don E. *Behavior Dynamics in Teaching, Learning and Growth*. Boston: Allyn and Bacon, 1975.

Hunt, J. McVicker. *Intelligence and Experience*. New York: Ronald Press Co., 1971.

Hurlock, Elizabeth B. *Child Development* (5th ed). New York: McGraw-Hill, 1972.

Jordan, Daniel C., and Streets, Donald T. "The Anisa Model: A New Basis for Educational Planning." *Young Children*, June 1973, pp. 290–307.

Kagan, Jerome. "Do the First Two Years Matter? A Conversation with Jerome Kagan." *Saturday Review of Education*, April 1973.

Kaluger, George, and Kaluger, Meriem Fair. *Human Development: The Span of Life*. St. Louis: The C. V. Mosby Co., 1974.

Langer, Jonas. *Theories of Development*. New York: Holt, Rinehart and Winston, 1969.

Liebert, Robert M. et al. *Developmental Psychology*. Englewood Cliffs, New Jersey: Prentice-Hall, 1977.

Ornstein, Robert E. *The Psychology of Consciousness*. San Francisco: W. H. Freeman and Co., 1972.

Papalia, Diane E., and Olds, Sally Wendkos. *A Child's World: Infancy through Adolescence*. New York: McGraw-Hill, 1975.

Piaget, Jean. *The Origins of Intelligence in Children*. New York: International Universities Press, 1952.

Stevens, Joseph H., Jr., and King, Edith W. *Administering Early Childhood Education Programs*. Boston: Little, Brown and Co., 1976.

Wadsworth, Barry J. *Processes of Cognitive Development*. New York: David McKay Co., 1971.

White, Robert W. "Motivation Reconsidered: The Concept of Competence." *Psychological Review*, 1959, *66*, 297–333.

ACTIVITIES

Report on the activities assigned by:

1. Writing a 3-5 page reaction paper.
2. Using another medium (tape, photography, drawing, etc.) with the instructor's consent.

1. Write an imaginary dialogue between a teacher trained in behaviorist theory and a teacher trained in cognitive-developmental theory, regarding what they think children are like and how they should be taught.

2. Observe a young child and interpret his behavior in terms of Erikson's stages of childhood development.

3. Observe a teacher presenting an activity to a child or group of children. What could you infer about the developmental theories she draws upon in her work with children?

4. Write a reflection about your own development. What forces seem to have been most significant (people, events, institutions, etc.)? How might these forces in your development influence your work with children?

DISCUSSION GUIDE

1.   What was your view of development before reading this chapter? Has it changed? How?

2.   Why might a teacher of young children need or want to know about the nature of theory?

3.   Of what value to the teacher is knowledge of developmental theories?

4.   What do you see as the best approach for a teacher to use in motivating children to learn in the classroom?

RESOURCES

Elkind, David. *Child Development and Education: A Piagetian Perspective.* New York: Oxford University Press, 1976.

_____. *A Sympathetic Understanding of the Child: Birth to Sixteen.* Boston: Allyn and Bacon, 1974.

Erikson, Erik. *Childhood and Society.* New York: Norton, 1950.

Flavell, John H. *Cognitive Development.* Englewood Cliffs, New Jersey: Prentice-Hall, 1977.

Gordon, Ira J. *Human Development from Birth through Adolescence* (2nd ed). New York: Harper and Row, 1969.

Hamachek, Don E. *Behavior Dynamics in Teaching, Learning, and Growth.* Boston: Allyn and Bacon, 1975.

Hunt, J. McVicker. *Intelligence and Experience.* New York: Ronald Press Co., 1971.

Jordan, Daniel C., and Streets, Donald T. "The Anisa Model: A New Basis for Educational Planning" Washington, D.C.: *Young Children,* June 1973, pp. 290–307.

Maslow, Abraham H. *Toward a Psychology of Being.* New York: Van Nostrand Reinhold, 1968.

Mead, Eugene D. *Six Approaches to Childrearing.* Provo, Utah: University of Brigham Young, 1976.

Nye, Robert D. *Three Views of Man.* Monterey, California: Brooks/ Cole Publishing Co., 1975.

Papalia, Diane E., and Olds, Sally Wendkos. *A Child's World: Infancy through Adolescence.* New York: McGraw-Hill, 1975.

Piaget, Jean. *The Origins of Intelligence in Children.* New York: International Universities Press, 1952.

Rogers, Carl R. *Client-Centered Therapy.* Boston: Houghton Mifflin Co., 1951.

Skinner, B. F. *Beyond Freedom and Dignity.* New York: Bantam Books, 1972.

Wadsworth, Barry J. *Processes of Cognitive Development.* New York: David McKay Co., 1971.

SELF-ASSESSMENT

After you have completed the reading, activities and small-group discussions, look again at the chapter objectives. Write a short paper responding to the following questions.

1. How would you describe your awareness, knowledge, and skill regarding the subject matter of this chapter before you began reading it and doing the activities?

2. To what extent do you feel that you have achieved each of the objectives presented at the beginning of the chapter?

3. What do you see as your strengths in this area?

4. In what specific areas do you need more information and experience? What kinds?

4

History and Models

This chapter is intended to provide an historical perspective to your developing role as a teacher of young children. In it, we sketch some historical background, describe some ways in which the past has influenced current thought and practice in early childhood education, and describe four major program models. Specifically, the objectives for this chapter are that you:

1. Become aware of the value of having an historical perspective on early childhood education.
2. Become aware of the roots of current practice in the humanistic tradition in education.
3. Become aware of the impact of recent social history on early childhood education.
4. Acquire knowledge of four program models which are influential in early childhood education today.

5. Begin to evaluate these program models in terms of your values and goals for children.

HISTORY AND MODELS

Knowledge of the history of educational thought gives teachers a sense of their roots in the past and contributes to understanding of current trends and issues. In this chapter we will give a brief overview of the history of early childhood education, designed to acquaint you, the prospective teacher, with the origins of some of the important ideas and practices found in programs today.

Knowledge of program models lets the teacher know the range of options available for her to choose from or adapt. Learning about and directly experiencing a variety of programs will enable you to see what kinds of curriculum techniques and teacher styles you feel most comfortable with and which you will want to adopt in your own teaching.

History History and tradition have directed the path of education, our understanding of where we are and where we are going, and our need to understand where we have come from. Historical perspectives give the teacher an idea of the sources of current philosophy, add to a sense of professional identity, and provide awareness that much of what is called *innovation* in current practice has been written about, and experimented with, before.

Early childhood education as a separate specialty did not begin until the early nineteenth century. However, many of the values and practices found in today's programs were created by philosophers, writers, and teachers in the past.

Today's developmental early childhood programs have their roots in what we refer to as the *humanistic* tradition in education. The theorists who contributed to this stream of thought were concerned with the education of the whole person, the interrelationships between mind and body, and the quality of the relationships between individuals. They supported education which fostered individual freedom and many of them supported universal education rather than educational opportunity only for the elite. Educators in the humanistic tradition tended to see childhood as a time to be enjoyed and education as a process to be enjoyed, rather than just preparation for adulthood.

The humanistic tradition stands in sharp contrast to the attitudes about children and education that were prevalent during the lifetime of the innovators. We will discuss their views, which were sometimes influential during their own time, but often regarded as radical and treated with suspicion and hostility.

In order to put historical discussion into perspective, it is useful to realize that childhood is a relatively new concept. During the Middle Ages children were regarded as small adults and given no special consideration or treatment. This is evident in the portrayal of children as miniature adults in the art of this period (Aries, 1962). A specialized field of early childhood education could not arise until there existed a concept of childhood as a unique developmental period. This concept did not emerge until the sixteenth and seventeenth centuries.

Historical Antecedents of Early Childhood Education

There have been some notable people in history whose ideas were especially significant in shaping today's educational thought. In this section we will describe philosophers and religious persons who addressed themselves not to early childhood education specifically, but to a total philosophy of education.

Many educational historians trace the humanistic tradition in education back to Plato (428–348 B.C.) and Aristotle (384–322 B.C.). Plato was concerned with developing an ethical and reasonable ruling class. Both Plato and Aristotle recognized the importance of beginning education with young children, both saw man as essentially good, emphasized the development of mind and body, and sought to create a society in which good men followed good laws.

Martin Luther (1483–1546), a religious leader during the Renaissance, was a strong advocate of universal education. He believed that in order for man to take responsibility for his own salvation, he would need to read and understand the Bible for himself.

Luther believed as well that the schools should develop the intellectual, religious, physical, emotional, and social qualities of children.

An extensive school system was developed in Germany in response to Luther's views but his goal of universal education did not become a reality until nineteenth century America.

John Amos Comenius (1592–1670) was a Czechoslovakian bishop, teacher, and educational theorist. Like Luther, he believed in universal education. He saw all people as being equal before God and believed, therefore, that all people, rich or poor, common or noble, male or female, were entitled to the same education.

Comenius stressed the importance of educating the young while they are tender and "can easily be bent and formed." He also advocated learning by doing and may have been the first to advocate learning through play.

He saw education as beginning at birth in "the school of the mother's knee" and extending throughout a lifetime of learning.

Jean Jacques Rousseau (1712–1778), French philosopher, writer, and social theorist, is remembered for his doctrine of the "noble savage." Rousseau's ideas about proper child rearing and education were a reaction to a corrupt government and society. Rousseau did not believe that man is born with original sin, but rather, that his inherent good is spoiled by civilization. In the novel *Émile*, Rousseau presents his view that the individual's innate goodness will flower when he is raised out of contact with corrupt society and is free to learn, not from books, but from direct contact with nature.

The Origins of Early Childhood Education

The educators whose theories are described in this section have had a direct impact on philosophy and practice in today's early childhood programs.

Pestalozzi

Some educational historians consider early childhood education as a distinct discipline to have had its beginning with

Johann Pestalozzi (1746–1827), a Swiss educational reformer. Pestalozzi was influenced by the ideas of Rousseau and decided upon a career in education after reading *Émile*. Like Luther and Comenius before him, he believed in education for all children.

Because of his love and concern for children and his belief that they need to be protected as well as educated, Pestalozzi devoted his life to education, particularly for the orphaned and poor. He set up schools where he could express his convictions and love for interacting with children.

Pestalozzi rejected the practice of memorization and advocated sensory exploration and observation as the basis of learning. Pestalozzi also believed in teaching human relationships. "My one aim was to ... awaken a feeling of brotherhood ... make them affectionate, just and considerate." (Braun, 1972, p. 52)

Froebel

Friedrich Wilhelm Froebel (1783–1852), a German, studied with Pestalozzi and was a teacher in one of his schools. Froebel was influenced by the ideas of Comenius and Rousseau, as well as Pestalozzi, and agreed with their view of man as innately good. Froebel believed that the child needed freedom to develop his natural capacity for goodness.

In Froebel's view, education was life for the child, not merely a preparation for adulthood. He saw the child as a social being, saw activity as the basis for knowing, and play as an essential part of education.

The kindergarten curriculum developed by Froebel included a set of *gifts* and *occupations* designed to enhance sensory development and to symbolically portray man's unity with God. The gifts consisted of objects like yarn balls, blocks, wooden tablets, natural objects, and geometric shapes which encouraged manipulation and discovery. Occupations included activities like molding, cutting, folding, bead stringing, and embroidery, which were intended to lead to skill development and inventiveness.

Froebel is considered the father of the modern kindergarten (children's garden) and, as such, he can be considered the father of modern early childhood education. Besides establishing the kindergarten, Froebel established an institute to train young women to become kindergarten teachers, a revolutionary idea in the early nineteenth century. Two of the women trained at his institute later established kindergartens in the United States, hence there is a direct link between Froebel and the American kindergarten.

Owen

Robert Owen (1771–1888), English social philosopher and controversial reformer, was another disciple of Pestalozzi. Owen became concerned with the poor conditions of families who worked in the cotton mills during the Industrial Revolution. He worked for reforms in the communities and established schools to improve the lives of children, who from the age of six worked long hours in the mills.

Owen believed that education, starting with the very young, combined with an environment which allowed people to live by the principle of mutual consideration, could transform the nature of people and society.

Owen's educational practices reflected his belief in the fundamental goodness of children. His infant school, the first in England for children three to ten years of age, had a warm, friendly atmosphere. Owen did not believe in pressuring children to learn nor in punishing them; rather, he showed children the negative consequences of their actions. Sensory learning, stories, audio-visual aids, and visitors from the community were included in the school program in an attempt to make school relevant and interesting to the children.

Owen's ideas were considered radical in his time, and his schools did not have lasting success in England. However, many of the practices originated in Owen's schools can still be found in today's early childhood programs, including periods of time during which children choose their activities; emphasis on a warm, nurturing and nonpunitive teacher role; and the use of spontaneous play as a vehicle for learning.

McMillan

Margaret McMillan (1860–1931) and her sister Rachel established the first nursery school in England in 1911. The school was created in response to the McMillans' concerns with the

health problems they witnessed in school-age children in poor communities. The nursery schools were designed to contribute to children's physical and mental development with a special emphasis on ameliorating health problems of very young children before they began formal schooling. Rachel McMillan died in 1917 a few years after the school began, but Margaret continued writing and teaching.

McMillan's nursery school provided for children's physical needs and placed heavy emphasis on allowing them to work and play outdoors. Health and nutrition, perceptual-motor skills, and the development of imagination were stressed. The role of the teacher in the program was to nurture children, to provide an environment for learning and informal teaching.

Many antecedents of today's nursery school were present in the early English nursery schools, including provision for sensory development, gardening, sand boxes, movement, nature study, play with creative materials like paint and blocks, and working with parents.

The English nursery school had a direct influence on the

development of early childhood education in the United States through several American pioneers in the field who went to England to study with McMillan.

Montessori

Maria Montessori (1870–1952), physician, reformer, educator, and feminist, was the first woman in Italy to receive a medical degree. She worked first with retarded children and later with normal children. She opened her first school the *Casa Dei Bambini* (Children's House) in 1907 in the Roman slum of San Lorenzo. This was followed by the opening of more schools and a training program for teachers.

Montessori believed that the universe was an orderly place and that children had an inherent desire to explore and understand the world in which they lived. Thus, she saw the learner as a young explorer setting out to make sense out of his environment and his own experiences. She saw this young explorer as largely self-motivating and seeking out the kinds of experiences and knowledge most appropriate for his current stage of development.

Montessori discarded many of the ways that her contemporaries looked at children and at learning. She was deeply concerned with preserving the dignity of the child, and she valued the development of independence and productiveness. The educational program she designed was based on her careful observation of young children, which led her to the conclusion that intelligence was not fixed and could be stimulated or stifled by the child's environment. She believed that the child learned best from his own direct sensory experience of the world.

Montessori used the first school at San Lorenzo as a laboratory for developing her curriculum. She began by creating an environment which was pleasant and child-size and teaching children to care for it. As she observed children interacting with the environment, she began to develop *didactic materials* to help children develop their senses and learn concepts. The development of these materials was influenced by earlier work by the French physicians Itard and Sequin, who had developed humane techniques for teaching retarded children.

The teachers in Montessori's first schools were not trained

teachers, but rather, were taught by Montessori to observe children carefully and respond to their observations. The role of the teacher (called *directress*) in a Montessori school is primarily one of observing and directing children to appropriate activities.

Montessori's schools were very successful in Italy and eventually spread throughout the world. Nursery schools in the United States adopted Montessori's ideas of creating a child-size environment and the use of sensory materials. Although there were a scattering of Montessori schools, her ideas did not have an impact in the United States until the 1960s when concern with the education of "disadvantaged" children gave her approach special relevance.

Today there are two major professional associations concerned with implementing Montessori programs, training teachers, and giving accreditation to schools and to teachers. These are the original organization, Association Montessori Internationale (AMI) with headquarters in the Netherlands, and the American Montessori Society (AMS) formed by Nancy McCormick Rambusch in New York in 1956 in order to adapt Montessori methods to an American style of working with children.

Early Childhood Education in America

John Dewey and Progressive Education

John Dewey (1859–1952) stands as a giant among modern educational theorists. Even though he was not primarily concerned with early childhood education, his influence has been so great that all areas of education in the United States have felt the impact of his work. His ideas have had a continued impact on the kindergarten and nursery school movement, which have always remained more closely allied with Dewey than with traditional public school systems.

Dewey's philosophy of education wove together ideas of

Comenius, Rousseau, Pestalozzi, and Froebel. He believed in respect for the child as a whole person, in a unified curriculum, and in self-directed activity. He felt strongly that education needed to be integrated with the child's life and should not be solely a preparation for future life.

Closely associated with Dewey is a movement called *progressive education*. Progressive education was a reaction against the traditional forms of public schooling prevalent during the nineteenth and early twentieth centuries in which children learned a set curriculum and skills by rote memorization under the strict discipline of the teacher.

Dewey became one of the best known spokespersons of the progressive movement. Progressive education took many forms based on a common set of principles which included the cultivation of individuality; child choice of activity; learning through experience; education as life, not just preparation for life; and learning as preparation for life in a rapidly changing world.

Progressive education came under increasing criticism during the 1940s and 1950s from educators who charged that students were not learning the fundamental subjects well enough. It is now commonly felt that Dewey was misinterpreted by many of his followers who interpreted his theories as implying permissiveness rather than development of self-direction and responsibility.

The Kindergarten Movement

Kindergartens in the United States developed independently from both the nursery school movement in England and elementary education. The first kindergarten in America was established in 1855 in Watertown, Wisconsin and was, like the others to follow, patterned after Froebel's kindergartens in Germany. The early kindergartens were started as private ventures, and many were directed by teachers trained in Froebel's methods.

The number of kindergartens expanded rapidly from 1870 to 1900. Two factors supported this rapid expansion. One factor was the growing belief that the inherent goodness of the child required a nurturing, benevolent environment to develop. The second factor was the spread of philanthropic social work. The earliest kindergarten teachers made home visits in the afternoons as social workers. Mission kindergartens for underprivileged children were often established as a part of settlement work with the hope that they would improve life for the future generation.

A period of ferment in the kindergarten began in the 1890s and lasted for 20 years. One group, known as the Progressives, was influenced by the work in child development, the current psychology, and the new philosophy stated by Dewey and others. The other group, the Conservatives, held to Froebelian principles and practices. By 1920 the conservative camp yielded and a new curriculum replaced the original curriculum designed by Froebel. The new kindergarten curriculum emphasized free play, social interaction, purposeful activity, art, music, nature study, and field excursions.

Kindergartens gradually moved into public schools, (the first in Saint Louis in the 1870s) where they met with grudging acceptance. The rigid atmosphere of the traditional primary schools with their emphasis on drill and the development of skills was sharply contrasted to the kindergartens which valued the development of the whole child and had a nonauthoritarian approach. However, the gap gradually narrowed. Many kindergarten activities found their way into the primary grades as did many primary activities filter down into the kindergarten.

Even today the debate about the proper role of the kindergarten continues between those who believe its purpose is to train children academically for success in later schooling and those who wish to preserve the spontaneity of learning through play.

The Nursery School Movement

The first nursery school in the United States was established in New York City in 1919 by Harriet Johnson. In the 1920s a number of other nursery schools were established in America. Some of the more notable ones included the Laboratory Nursery School at Columbia Teachers College organized by Patty Smith Hill, a strong advocate of progressive education in the kindergarten, and the Ruggles Street Nursery School and Training Center in Boston, directed by Abigail Eliot, who studied with Margaret McMillan in England.

During the 1920s and 1930s, nursery school programs grew. Many were established as laboratories for studying child development, and some were connected with teacher training programs. These early nursery schools emphasized primarily the social, emotional, and physical growth of the child.

During the Depression, the government sponsored WPA (Works Projects Administration) nurseries, and during World War II, sponsored day care centers to provide child care for working mothers. Private industry also sponsored day care. Kaiser shipyards, for example, ran two outstanding child care centers. After World War II was over and women were no longer badly needed on the labor market, many of the private and all of the federally operated centers shut down.

Child care services between 1945 and 1960 received little support. The post-war baby boom and the feminine mystique emphasized the role of the woman in the home. Also contributing to the lack of support for child care programs was the belief which was prevalent at the time that children of working mothers suffered from a lack of essential maternal care and love. While there was little support for day care services for children of working parents, the traditional university connected or privately supported, half-day nursery school programs continued to serve mainly middle-class families.

Head Start and Follow Through

Interest in programs for young children has grown tremendously over the last two decades in the United States. The launch of the Russian Sputnik in 1957 generated national concern that American children were not being adequately educated to compete in a scientific age. This concern, combined with research by Piaget, Hunt, Bloom, and others on the significance of the early years on intellectual development, led to increased research and a proliferation of programs for young children.

Most notable of these is project *Head Start*—a federally funded program designed to counteract the effects of deprivation on the development of poor children. Head Start, a demonstration program administered first by the Office of Economic Opportunity and then by the U.S. Office of Child Development, focuses on the total development of the child in the context of his family. In addition to an educational component, Head Start programs have provision for social and psychological services, medical and dental screening and treatment, and a nutrition program. Parent involvement is stressed heavily and includes both participation in the classroom to learn skills in facilitating children's development, and opportunity for parents to participate in program policy and decision making. Head Start continues as a demonstration program and has had an important impact on subsequent federal programs and on proposed national child care legislation.

In 1968 the Office of Child Development authorized an experimental program called *Planned Variation* to investigate the effects of a variety of curricular approaches in Head Start programs. During the school year 1969–1970, a pilot program was initiated to test the effectiveness of a number of educational models. Another new program, called *Follow Through,* was introduced in 1969 by the U.S. Office of Education in response to hasty research which indicated that gains achieved in the Head Start program were lost when children entered public school. The intent of the Follow Through program was to continue intervention programs for Head Start children after they entered elementary school. The same experimental models used in the Head Start Planned Variation Study were continued in selected districts in kindergarten through third grade. An effort was made to coordinate the programs so that children attended classes employing the same curricular model from preschool through third grade.

The Planned Variation study included a number of educational models which varied greatly in theory and practice and represented a spectrum of approaches to early childhood education. Each model was developed by a program sponsor, usually based in a university or educational research center, who developed an educational program for children and techniques for training teachers to use the program. Some of the models have developed curriculum and materials which have been adopted and are being used in a variety of settings today.

Following is a brief description of some of the best known of these experimental programs.

The *Bank Street Model,* sponsored by Bank Street College in New York City, emphasizes a child development approach, the integration of subject areas through learning trips, and has as its primary goal that the child become self-directed in his learning.

The *Tucson Early Education Model* (TEEM), developed by Ronald Henderson and Marie Hughes at the University of Arizona, focuses on the development of skills and attitudes, especially in the area of language development. The program emphasizes imitation of behavioral models and the use of social reinforcement to ensure the child experiences frequent success.

The *Cognitively Oriented Curriculum* developed by David Weikart in Ypsilanti, Michigan, is based on Piaget's theories and includes visits to the home where the teachers work with parents to promote children's cognitive growth as well as a center-based cognitive curriculum.

The *Florida Project,* sponsored by Ira Gordon at University of Florida, works with infants as well as young children. Parent educators from the community are trained to demonstrate tasks that parents can use to foster social and intellectual skills in their children.

The *Responsive Environment Model,* developed at the Far West Laboratory for Educational Research and Development in San Francisco, aims to help children to develop both positive self-image and intellectual ability. The environment is designed to be responsive to the child, and learning activities are designed to be intrinsically motivating and self-rewarding.

The model developed by *Education Development Center* in Cambridge, Massachusetts, is based on the British Infant School. Class activities arise from the needs and interests of the children, rather than a prescribed curriculum. The role of the teacher is to guide children and structure the environment.

The academically oriented program, developed by *Engelmann and Becker* at University of Oregon, teaches language, reading, and math skills. The structured approach utilizes programmed materials and systematic reinforcement of positive responses.

The *Behavior Analysis Model,* developed by Don Bushell at the University of Kansas, has as its goal teaching children needed skills by means of systematic reinforcement procedures. The teacher's role is that of a behavior modifier.

The primary goal of the Planned Variation and Follow Through research was to evaluate the relative effectiveness of these and other program models. The research to date indicates that children in the academically oriented programs which employ behavior modification practices have made the greatest gains on standardized measures of intellectual achievement. There are problems in interpreting these research findings, however, because we do not have reliable measures for goals of programs which stress self-concept and self-directed learning. Although the research evidence is not conclusive, this study has focused national attention on early childhood curriculum, heightened awareness of the impact of different educational practices, and has resulted in the introduction of innovative programs in the public schools.

Earlier research findings which indicated that preschool intervention program gains were lost when the children entered elementary school have been contradicted by new research conclusions that suggest that intervention programs do have far reaching impact on IQ scores and skill development. Researchers have identified what they refer to as a "sleeper effect"—improved performance which becomes apparent several years after the child enters elementary school (Report on Preschool Education, May 15, 1977).

Types of Programs in Operation Today

Today, interest in early childhood education programs continues to grow. More widespread means of birth control, the Women's Liberation Movement, economic necessity, and new awareness that children can develop normally even when they are not reared exclusively by their mothers, all combine to increase the number of working mothers and the demand for quality child care.

A number of different types of programs for young children exist today. These may be classified according to their purpose—to provide child care for working parents, to provide for the education and development of the child or a combination of the two.

Programs which are designed to provide care for children of working parents can be *custodial* or *developmental* in nature. Custodial programs provide a minimal program for children which can range from warm, caring, homelike settings, to parking lots for children where there is little concern for their development. Developmental programs, which provide an educational program stimulating intellectual development, are concerned with all other areas of the child's development as well. These programs often include medical and social services and provision for parent involvement.

Half-day nursery school programs, often sponsored by churches, university child development laboratories, and parent cooperative arrangements, focus on the development of the child through enrichment experiences and tend to serve middle-class families who do not need full-day care to enable mothers to work.

Programs may also be classified according to sponsorship, which may be public (federal government, state or local agency) or private. Federal programs include Head Start and programs funded by Title XX (originally Title IV-A) of the 1937 Social Security Act. The purpose of Title XX programs is to enable income eligible parents to work, to receive job training, or to relieve families from stress. The intent of federally funded programs is to support the family through comprehensive services.

Privately sponsored programs include church programs, both full and part day; programs sponsored by industry for their employees; and profit and nonprofit programs run by individuals and groups.

Family day care homes are the least visible yet most prevalent forms of privately sponsored child care used by parents in the United States today. These programs are run by women who care for small numbers of infants, toddlers, and preschool children in their homes. A good family day care home is appropriate for a young child who functions best in a small, homelike setting.

Models

Differences among programs for young children can also be looked at in terms of the way educational philosophy is translated into practice. Each program adopts knowingly or unknowingly one or several approaches to education. We will use the word *model* to describe these different approaches. For our purpose, the term *model* includes a systematic approach to curriculum and teaching. A model is made up of many interrelated parts. These parts include philosophy, goals and objectives, teacher role (including strategies and methods), structure of the educational environment, content, and materials.

Underlying each model are assumptions about the nature of society, the nature of learning and the learner, and the purpose of education. Whether these assumptions are stated or only implied, they form the base upon which the goals and objectives of the model rest. No one model has been shown to be superior to others. A good program is one which is good for the teacher and the children being taught and reflects the values and goals of the teacher and parents.

Knowledge of models provides an organized, systematic base for examining and developing programs. Without such a base, a program can become an incoherent and even self-contradictory collection of bits and pieces. As a prospective teacher, you can pick and choose among existing models, seeing which are compatible with your personality and values, and then design your own program, adopting and modifying models to fit your situation. Models can also provide the base from which you can continuously evaluate and revise your program in a way consistent with your values and goals.

We will conclude this chapter by describing four of the major models of early childhood education. We have chosen these four models because they are the source of many of the practices we see in classrooms today. Two of the models, the Montessori model and programs based on behavior modification, have been developed in great detail. The others, the traditional nursery school and the informal British infant school, provide more general guidelines for teaching based on a set of beliefs about learning. We will discuss these models in terms of their underlying assumptions, goals, teacher role, classroom organization, and curriculum.

Montessori

Montessori believed that the basis for learning was firsthand experience. Thus, she designed her educational approach so that children learned through observing and doing. Practical life experiences such as buttoning, zipping, cutting, polishing, and gardening enabled children to care for themselves and the environment and provided the foundation for the rest of the program. Sensory experiences provided through *didactic materials* designed by Montessori helped children develop the ability to concentrate, the ability to differentiate their sense perceptions, and concepts of size, shape, color, texture, sound, and temperature. Conceptual learning through didactic materials extended into other areas including writing, reading, and mathematics. Development of feelings of self-esteem arose in the child as he increased his competence in all areas of his life.

The beautifully designed and crafted didactic materials are the best known aspect of Montessori's educational approach. The materials are graded by ability, sequenced from known to unknown, and from concrete to abstract. The concept to be taught by each material is isolated from other concepts which might be confusing or distracting. For example, if the child is learning the concept of shape, the materials will be of uniform size and color so that the attribute of shape will be isolated. Materials are also designed to have immediate self-correcting feedback so the child can see if he has successfully completed

the task without being dependent on the teacher to tell him.

Montessori stressed the importance of an orderly environment which helped children to focus on their learning and develop the ability to concentrate. The physical environment in a Montessori classroom is attractive, child-size, and equipped with movable furniture. Materials are treated with care and respect and are displayed so that children can use them independently.

The role of the teacher in a Montessori program is to create the environment, to be a model for learning and human relationships, and to observe each child in order to determine his level of development and to guide him to work with materials that match his readiness. Each learning exercise is introduced by the teacher to the child, or small group of children, who are ready for it. Children then work independently (or with a friend) on the exercises, each of which has a preparation phase, a work period, and a putting away phase. Children work with the material in the way it was presented by the teacher until she can see that they have mastered the concept to be learned. When the child has acquired the concept, the teacher may introduce variations in the way the material can be used.

All learning in a Montessori classroom is based on a foundation of what has gone before so that each activity paves the way to future, more complex activities. Activities are organized primarily for individual work rather than group interaction, and children are allowed to move freely about the environment and make their own choices about the activities they wish to engage in.

There are a number of very different interpretations of Montessori's philosophy. Some teachers use only materials designed by Montessori in their classrooms and follow her prescriptions exactly, while others add new materials and develop variations based on the resources in their environments and their particular situation.

Traditional Nursery School

The American nursery school developed out of very different sources than the traditional, Prussian-based, and highly formalized elementary school. It combined the early English nursery schools with Freudian thought, which was influential in

the United States in the early part of the twentieth century.

In the traditional nursery school the child learns through interactions with people and the environment. He is seen as a person in transition—always growing, changing, experiencing. The role of the school is to keep the paths of exploration open to the child so that he can best develop in his own way. In the traditional nursery school a heavy emphasis is placed on the child's social and emotional development.

The role of the teacher in the nursery school is to create an environment which facilitates learning. The teacher observes children and interacts with them in ways that foster their development. An important aspect of the program is to facilitate social and emotional development by encouraging children to verbalize their feelings. Child management is carried out by problem solving and by modifying the environment rather than by imposing adult power. The teacher has a teaching plan, but she is ready to modify that plan if it does not seem suitable for the children's needs at a particular time.

The daily schedule in a traditional nursery school is characterized by large time blocks in which the child is free to choose his own activities and engage in them for as long as he wishes. The children may all come together for group activities such as snack, story, music, or movement. The classroom is divided into activity areas usually including an area for blocks, dramatic play, art, water play, sand, and books.

The traditional nursery school is like the Montessori approach in that both see the child as an inquisitive, self-motivated learner progressing through developmental stages in which he selects from the environment those things that are appropriate to his current needs. It differs from the Montessori approach in that it places greater emphasis on self-expression (both creative expression and the verbalization of feelings) and on open-ended materials which the child can choose to use in a variety of ways.

In response to new information about cognitive development and to the needs of low income children, the traditional nursery school has continued to evolve, especially in the area of intellectual development and learning. What remains constant is the insistence that the child is a person in the process of developing and whose development can be supported by a sensitive teacher in a carefully designed environment.

Behavior Modification

Programs based on behavior modification differ fundamentally from the other models described in that they do not come out of a humanistic educational tradition. Their source is the area of psychology called *learning theory,* which is based on principles of stimulus-response. This approach emphasizes the use of reinforcements to promote predetermined behaviors.

Behavior modification applied to teaching is not restricted to any particular age group or subject matter. In the field of early childhood education, it has been used both as a tool for behavior management and as a teaching technique, especially in programs for children who are retarded or have problems in learning.

The value of behavior modification in teaching lies in the fact that it demands clearly stated behavioral goals and a definite plan of instruction that begins at whatever level the learner is able to respond to. It is a very active approach requiring continual response from the learner and immediate feedback from the teacher (or the teaching material). If the learner is unable to correctly respond, the teacher backs up to a point where the learner is able to respond correctly. Ideally, every learner is able to reach a clearly defined behavioral goal and experience success.

Programs for young children using a behaviorist approach include the Behavior Analysis Follow Through Program, developed by Don Bushell at the University of Kansas, and *Distar,* a commercially produced program based on the Follow Through Model, developed by Sigfried Engelmann and Wesley Becker.

The teacher role in a behavior modification program such as *Distar* is strictly programmed. The teacher has little room to make decisions, and thus, has little creative input into the program. The program, however, does demand that the teacher play a very active role in providing continual stimuli and feedback to the students.

The *Distar* program itself is relatively easy to implement, since it is basically a self-contained kit which gives the teacher specific directions. Typically, the students spend an intense 20–30 minute a day period in which the curriculum is directly taught. Pretesting is usually required since the materials assume a relatively homogeneous group of learners. The approach requires constant feedback and correction; therefore, it must be used with small groups, usually 5–8 students at a time.

The basic assumptions of the behaviorist approach differ radically from the assumptions underlying all the other models described in this chapter. Perhaps the key point of difference between the behavior modification approach, on the one hand, and the various programs within the humanistic educational tradition, on the other, is the role of the learner and the teacher. In the behavior modification approach the learner plays a *passive* role with motivation viewed as coming from external sources; in the humanistic approaches the learner is *active* and seen as internally motivated. By active and passive we do not mean the amount of minute-by-minute physical or verbal activity the learner is engaged in, but whether the learner himself shapes and controls what is learned or whether teaching process shapes and controls what is learned.

The behavior modification approach has limitations in that it places both the teacher and the learner in rather mechanical roles. The behavior or information acquired may be very specific and not easily generalized; hence, it may be a meaningless trick from the standpoint of the child in much the same way that teaching a parrot to talk is a meaningless trick to the parrot. The behaviorist approach concentrates on producing a limited range of behavior in a teacher-structured situation rather than on supporting the growth that the individual finds most rewarding. Nevertheless, it is a mistake to dismiss behaviorist approaches to education lightly. They demand that a teaching program set clear goals and have a specific plan for moving the learner along step by step until these goals are reached.

British Infant School

In England the state supported educational system for children between the ages of 5 and 7 is known as the *infant school.* In the period after World War II, a new approach evolved in the infant schools called the *open school,* the *integrated day,* or *informal education.* This approach, or more accurately, this collection of similar approaches, came to public attention both in England and the United States, through the publication of a governmental study, *Children and their Primary Schools*, also known as the Plowden Report (Silberman, 1970).

The British infant school is sometimes called an open school, both in the sense that the use of space is "open" (for example, no fixed desks and children are free to move from area to area), and in the sense that the content is open, that is, it derives from interests children are engaged in rather than from a pre-set curriculum that prescribes subject matter in fixed time blocks. This approach to organization is often referred to as the integrated day. Activities or skills are not divided into specific subject areas and scheduled at specific times except for a few fixed periods such as music and movement, assembly, and lunch.

Like the traditional nursery school, the British infant school drew heavily on the philosophy of John Dewey. The development of the infant school was also greatly influenced by the work of Jean Piaget, which emphasized that children play the central role in their own learning and that they go through developmental stages in their intellectual growth.

Educators who use this approach believe that children must make sense of the world around them in their own way, through their own exploration. They must themselves "Gradually develop concepts of causal relationships, the power to discriminate, to make judgments, to analyze and synthesize, to imagine and to formulate" (Plowden Report, in Silberman, 1970, p. 219).

The way that children do this is through play. "Play is the principal means through which children reconcile their inner lives with external reality.... We know now that play—in the sense of 'messing around' either with material objects or with other children and of creating fantasies—is vital to children's learning, and therefore vital in school" (Plowden Report, Silberman, 1970, p. 219).

The British infant school is part of the regular school system. It has broken with the formal traditional primary education, but it has not fundamentally altered the goals of the educational system which are to develop competency in the basic skills of communication (oral language, reading, and writing) and mathematics. However, the British infant school does place a stronger emphasis on physical development through creative movement experiences than the traditional program did.

In more general terms, the British infant school aims at producing happy, cheerful, well-balanced children, who are intellectually alive and curious and who have respect for others. Compared with American schools, there is much more emphasis in the British infant school on producing children who are able to express personal ideas and feelings fluently and imaginatively.

Children play the central role in their own learning, and the role of the teacher in the British infant school is to support and extend the child's exploration of the world. The teacher must carefully observe children and provide the kinds of experiences appropriate to the needs of the individual child. It is the teacher's responsibility to provide experiences that lead to achieving educational goals. Children are in school for a purpose. As the Plowden Report puts it, "From the start, there must be teaching as well as learning: children are not 'free' to develop interests or skills of which they have no knowledge. They must have guidance from their teachers" (Silberman, 1970, p. 209). Thus in the British infant school, the teacher is the middleman who links together the individual personalities and abilities of the children with the educational objectives of the school. On the whole, the teachers are given great freedom (with its accompanying responsibility) as to the means they will employ in their classrooms to meet educational goals.

In order to reach their objectives, teachers in the British infant school have radically reorganized the classroom use of time and space. In traditional classrooms, time is a more important organizing factor than space. The British infant school uses space rather than time as the organizing principle of the classroom. The typical classroom is divided into a number of interest areas; for example, a reading corner, a math center, an art center, an area for building things, and a dramatic play area. Classrooms also contain areas for block, sand, and water play. Children have a great deal of freedom to work in the interest area that they choose. Since children in each area proceed at their own pace, conventional time-based curriculum (50 minutes for reading, 30 for social studies) is inappropriate.

The second major reorganization of the classroom in the British infant school is a shift in the structure of the curriculum. Most schools and most classrooms are organized around subject matter—art, reading, social studies, mathematics. Each of these subject areas require the learner to perform special tasks or activities. Another way of organizing education programs is to subordinate the subject matter to an organizing interest or project. In the British infant school, the subject matter being taught often grows out of the child's experience with certain tasks or projects. For example, if children set out with a task of building a birdhouse, they need to engage with a number of subject areas (reading, math, science, etc.) in order to accomplish their purpose. The great advantage of this approach is that it begins with a concrete problem that the child is attempting to solve. The problem-based approach is ideally suited to the interest area design of the British infant school. Certain problems can be prearranged, but others grow out of the ongoing activities of the child himself under the constant monitoring and direction of the teacher.

The British infant schools have sometimes been confused with the "free" school movement. The free school movement in the United States differs from the open or informal school in that free schools takes place outside the publicly supported education system. Free schools do not necessarily accept conventional educational goals which stress intellectual development (in fact, free schools are often started by parents who are in radical disagreement with the goals of the public educational system); and they typically give the child a great degree of choice and freedom.

REFERENCES

Aries, Philippe. *Centuries of Childhood.* New York: Vintage Books, 1962.

Auleta, Michael S. *Foundations of Early Childhood Education.* New York: Random House, 1969.

Braun, Samuel J., and Edwards, Esther P. *History and Theory of Early Childhood Education.* Belmont, California: Wadsworth Publishing Co., 1972.

Clegg, Sir Alex. *Revolution in the British Primary Schools.* Washington, D.C.: National Education Association, 1971.

Dewey, John. *Experience and Education.* New York: Collier Books, 1972.

Engelmann, Sigfried, and Bereiter, Carl. *Teaching Disadvantaged Children in the Preschool.* Englewood Cliffs, New Jersey: Prentice-Hall, 1966.

Featherstone, Joseph. *Schools Where Children Learn.* New York: Liveright, 1971.

Frost, Joe L., and Kissinger, Joan B. *The Young and the Educative Process.* New York: Holt, Rinehart and Winston, 1976.

Hess, Robert, and Croft, Doreen J. *Teachers of Young Children* (2nd ed.). Boston: Houghton Mifflin, 1975.

Joyce, Bruce, and Weil, Marsha. *Models of Teaching.* Englewood Cliffs, New Jersey: Prentice-Hall, 1972.

Maccoby, Eleanor E., and Zellner, Miriam. *Experiments in Primary Education: Aspects of Project Follow-Through.* New York: Harcourt Brace Jovanovich, 1970.

MacDonald, James B. Introduction. *A New Look at Progressive Education,* James R. Squire, (Ed.). Washington, D.C.: Association for Supervision and Curriculum Development, 1972.

Montessori, Maria. *Dr. Montessori's Own Handbook.* New York: Schocker Books, 1965.

———. *The Absorbent Mind.* New York: Holt, Rinehart and Winston, 1967.

Neill, A. S. *Summerhill: A Radical Approach to Childrearing.* New York: Hart Publishing Co., 1960.

Read, Katherine, *The Nursery School: A Human Relations Laboratory* (6th ed.). Philadelphia: W. B. Saunders Co., 1976.

Report on Preschool Education, vol. 9, March 1977. Washington, D.C.: Education News Services Division of Capital Publications, 1977.

Silberman, Charles E. *Crisis in the Classroom.* New York: Random House, 1970.

Spodek, Bernard, *Early Childhood Education.* Englewood Cliffs, New Jersey: Prentice-Hall, 1973.

Standing, E. M. *Maria Montessori: Her Life and Work.* Fresno, Calif.: Academy Library Guild, 1959.

Weber, Evelyn. *The Kindergarten: Its Encounter with Educational Thought in America.* New York: Teacher's College Press, 1969.

Weber, Lillian. *The English Infant School and Informal Education.* Englewood Cliffs, New Jersey: Prentice-Hall, 1971.

ACTIVITIES

Report on the activities assigned by:

1. Writing a 3–5 page reaction paper.
2. Using another medium (tape recorder, photography, drawing, etc.) with the instructor's consent.

1. What were your impressions from reading the section on the history of early childhood education? What implications did you find for your role as a teacher of young children?

2. Which of the models described seems closest to your values and the ways you would like to work with children? How does it relate to your values and why do you feel you might be comfortable working in that way?

3. How could programs you have observed and worked in be classified in terms of their purpose and sponsorship? To what extent did they provide comprehensive services for children? What were your feelings about the strengths and weaknesses of each program?

4. If these activities do not challenge you or provide for growth, design your own activity with the consent of the instructor.

DISCUSSION GUIDE

1. Why might a teacher of young children need or want to know about the history of early childhood education?

2. Why might a teacher of young children need or want to know about different program models in early childhood education?

3. Have you observed programs which incorporate any aspects of the models described in this chapter? What were your impressions of them?

RESOURCES

Auleta, Michael S. *Foundation of Early Childhood Education*. New York: Random House, 1969.

Braun, Samuel J., and Edwards, Esther P. *History and Theory of Early Childhood Education*. Belmont, California: Wadsworth Publishing Co., 1972.

Clegg, Sir Alex. *Revolution in the British Primary Schools*. Washington, D.C.: National Education Association, 1971.

Dewey, John. *Experience and Education*. New York: Collier Books, 1972.

Engelmann, Sigfried, and Bereiter, Carl. *Teaching Disadvantaged Children in the Preschool*. Englewood Cliffs, New Jersey: Prentice-Hall, 1966.

Featherstone, Joseph. *Schools Where Children Learn*. New York: Liveright, 1971.

Frost, Joe L., and Kissinger, Joan B. *The Young Child and the Educative Process*. New York: Holt, Rinehart, and Winston, 1976.

Maccoby, Eleanor E., and Zellner, Miriam. *Experiments in Primary Education: Aspects of Project Follow-Through*. New York: Harcourt Brace Jovanovich, 1970.

Montessori, Maria. *Dr. Montessori's Own Handbook*. New York: Schocken Books, 1965.

_____. *The Absorbent Mind*. New York: Holt, Rinehart and Winston, 1967.

Neill, A. S. *Summerhill: A Radical Approach to Childrearing*. New York: Hart Publishing Co., 1960.

Read, Katherine. *The Nursery School: A Human Relations Laboratory* (6th ed.). Philadelphia: W. B. Saunders Co., 1976.

Silberman, Charles E. *Crisis in the Classroom*. New York: Random House, 1970.

Spodek, Bernard. *Early Childhood Education*. Englewood Cliffs, New Jersey: Prentice-Hall, 1973.

Standing, E. M. *Maria Montessori: Her Life and Work*. Fresno, Calif.: Academy Library Guild, 1959.

Weber, Evelyn. *The Kindergarten: Its Encounter with Educational Thought in America*. New York: Teachers College Press, 1969.

Weber, Lillian. *The English Infant School and Informal Education*. Englewood Cliffs, New Jersey: Prentice-Hall, 1971.

SELF-ASSESSMENT

After you have completed the reading, activities, and small-group discussions, look again at the chapter objectives. Write a short paper responding to the following questions.

1. How would you describe your awareness, knowledge, and skill regarding the subject matter of this chapter before you began reading it and doing the activities?

2. To what extent do you feel that you have achieved each of the objectives presented at the beginning of the chapter?

3. What do you see as your strengths in this area?

4. In what specific areas do you need more information and experience? What kinds?

5

Observation

PURPOSE AND OBJECTIVES

This chapter is designed to make you aware of the importance of observation as a tool for teachers of young children. In it, we discuss the process of observation and its purposes, and give guidelines for developing observation skills. Specifically, the objectives of this chapter are that you:

1. Become aware of the importance of observation in an early childhood program.

2. Become aware of the usefulness of focusing observation on children, on classrooms, and on personal feelings and reactions.

3. Develop understanding of the observation process.

4. Develop skill in writing clear and objective descriptions of children, their behavior and interactions.

5. Develop skill in interpreting behavior based on observable data.

6. Become aware of your own feelings and reactions to what you observe and able to separate these from description and interpretation.
7. Develop ability to use observation skills to examine your own interactions with children and adults.
8. Understand the uses of different systematic observation techniques in your work with children.

OBSERVATION

One of the most important skills that a teacher of young children can develop is the ability to observe. Observation is more than casual looking; it means gathering information and impressions with a mind that is open and unprejudiced.

Through observing carefully and objectively teachers gain invaluable information and understanding. Observation is the basis of much of what they do in working with children and is used in some form in every area discussed in this book. For not only do teachers observe children and classrooms but they observe themselves—their values, their strengths and weaknesses in relating to others, and the choices they make.

Areas of Observation The teacher of young children will find it useful to focus observations on three subjects: children, classrooms, and personal feelings and reactions.

Observation of Children

The first, and most important, subject for a teacher's observation is children. The primary focus of this chapter is to help you develop observation skills. Careful observation will help you to know children and to plan and make decisions in the classroom. It will also help you communicate the child's developmental progress to parents, teachers, administrators, and other professionals who might be involved in helping the child.

An effective teacher of young children has the ability to wait and see what is happening. Such "intensive waiting" (Nyberg, 1971, p. 168) can take the form of objective observation, which

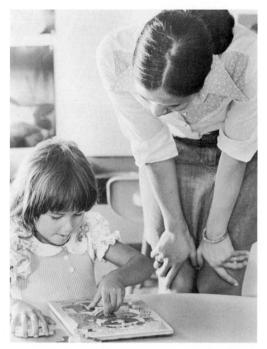

requires that you suspend your expectations and simply be receptive to what *is*—feelings, behaviors, and patterns. This doesn't mean that you must become an impersonal machine like a robot; it does require you to carefully separate what was observed from what you might have wanted or from what you feared.

Through observation, teachers learn a number of different things about children and their learning.

- Observation of children provides the teacher with increased sensitivity to how children behave, think, and feel and with heightened awareness of the unique qualities of each individual child and the world of children.
- The teacher can assess the developmental level of the children she works with through careful observation and compare her data to developmental norms. In this way the teacher verifies her knowledge of child growth and development.

- Observation assists the teacher in understanding individual behavior problems. She can gather information through observation of the child's behavior interaction with materials and the items he produces such as paintings, clay objects, and construction. The data can be used to develop hypotheses regarding the nature of the problem and possible solutions.

- The teacher can observe children's interests, skills, strengths, and weaknesses, and plan activities based on this information. She can then observe the children's responses to the activities planned and evaluate their effectiveness in accomplishing her learning objectives. Observation as a basis for curriculum planning is discussed in Chapter 8, "Designing Learning Experiences."

A valuable function of observation in working with young children is one we discovered through an assignment we gave in a college class. We designed an activity to increase students' skill in observation and description. We brought a bowl of four goldfish to class and had each student choose one fish to observe and describe. We did not have time to complete the activity and intended to resume it on Monday. Unfortunately two of the fish did not survive the weekend.

When we gave the students the sad news that two of the fish had died they all responded spontaneously with distress and concern, "Which ones?" At that moment we realized an important thing about observation—it encourages a relationship of empathy, caring, and concern!

Observation of Learning Environments

By focusing your observation on selected aspects of a complex, busy classroom you can evaluate the effectiveness of the physical setting and the dynamics of the relationships within it. This type of observation helps you to generate ideas about how to improve the learning environment.

The value of individual observations can be enhanced when an entire staff compares their observations to get more in-depth understanding of the effectiveness of the physical environment. In one of the schools we work with, the staff frequently meets to evaluate how well the classroom arrangement supports their goals for the children. When they observe problems—blocks being tripped over, open pathways that encourage running, reading areas that are too near noisy activities—they spend a Saturday morning moving the furniture and redesigning the environment. Then the observation process begins again.

Observation of Personal Feelings and Reactions

The third subject for observation is yourself. As you watch your own behavior and interactions, you develop greater awareness and knowledge of how you feel and respond in various situations and the impact of your behavior on others. Awareness gained through self-observation is a necessary first step in enabling you to make choices about how to respond in any situation.

The Observation Process

Observation is the process of watching closely and recording what you see. You can organize your observations of children and classrooms to pay special attention to those things you wish to learn more about. Your knowledge of human growth and development, when combined with careful observation, will often provide clues for understanding behavior and guiding children's development. In order to help our students develop skill in observation we divided the process into three parts:

1. Description
2. Interpretation based on what is seen.
3. Acknowledgment of feelings and reactions.

Description. The first, and most essential step in observation is to look closely and describe as carefully as possible what you see. Objective observation is dependent on experiencing as completely as possible while suspending interpretation and judgment. Objectivity means seeing what is actually taking place. It means observing without making value judgments like "bad" or "good" or "right" or "wrong." It means trying to reduce the distortions that are the result of biases or defenses or preconceptions (Read, 1976, pp. 124–125).

Objectivity is difficult because you are a participant in the life of the classroom you observe and therefore you have influence on the people in it and are influenced by them. If you are aware of your impact on the situation and its impact on you, you can work toward careful and unbiased descriptions.

Skill in writing observations of children develops through practice and more practice. Good observations use clear language and communicate enough information to convey the uniqueness of the subject of the observation. It is useful to write soon after the observation is made in order to retain the clarity of your impressions.

Interpretation. The second basic step in the classroom observation process is to make interpretations based on what you have seen. While behavior is observable and can be described more or less objectively, the sources of behavior are not visible and may only be inferred. You need to observe closely, describe

carefully, and then seek the relationship between the observed behavior and its unobservable cause. While you can never truly know why a child behaves as he does, as a teacher you will make decisions based on your assumptions about children's behavior every day.

When your interpretations are based on careful and complete description, it is possible for others to examine the data and decide whether or not they agree with your interpretation. This gives you the benefit of their insight and offers the opportunity for more creative solutions based on the collective experience of all who review your observation.

Interpreting child behavior is difficult because so many factors—stage of development, health, cultural influences, and individual experience—combine in complex ways to determine how a child acts in a given situation. The same behavior can mean very different things in different children, and different observers may interpret the same behavior or incident in totally different ways. For example, several of our college students noticed a little girl who was lying in a large cement pipe in the yard of a preschool we were visiting. When asked to interpret the meaning of the child's behavior one student thought that she was withdrawn and antisocial, another was convinced that she was lonely, unhappy, and in need of comforting, and the third felt that she was just taking a few moments for quiet contemplation. Obviously the students were drawing hasty conclusions based on minimal information. They needed more information about the child and the events which preceded their observation in order to make more accurate and meaningful interpretations.

Acknowledgment of Feelings and Reactions. The third step in the observation process is to notice and acknowledge the feelings and reactions that may have come up in the course of observing. You may have strong feelings or reactions to the children and situations you observe. Responding with feeling is a natural part of our experience. Reporting your feelings and reactions separate from description and interpretation gives you the opportunity to share your personal responses without distorting the observation. Your reactions provide a personal context which can help the reader understand the situation.

Figure 5, titled The Observation Process, illustrates the in-

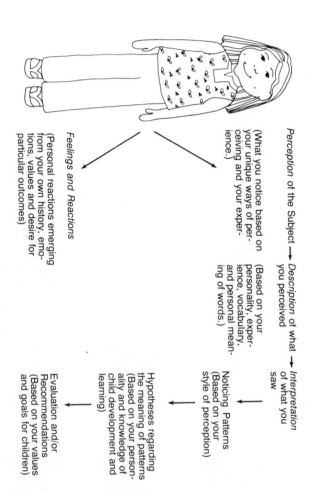

Perception of the Subject → Description of what you perceived → Interpretation of what you saw

(What you notice based on your unique ways of perceiving and your experience.)

(Based on your personality, experience, vocabulary, and personal meaning of words.)

Feelings and Reactions
(Personal reactions emerging from your own history, emotions, values and desire for particular outcomes)

Noticing Patterns
(Based on your style of perception)

Hypotheses regarding the meaning of patterns
(Based on your personality and knowledge of child development and learning)

Evaluation and/or Recommendations
(Based on your values and goals for children)

Figure 5. *The Observation Process.*

terrelatedness of the components of observation and how the history and personality of the observer influence this process.

Developing Skill in Writing Observations

To master the skill of writing good observations takes time, commitment, and practice. While almost everybody can agree on an observation that vividly portrays a sense of a child or an interaction, it is difficult to do more than make broad generalizations about how to write a good observation. In what follows we present some guidelines that have aided our students to develop skills in writing observations and critically examining their writing. These are intended to help you learn to write observations. We urge you to develop a style of writing that pleases you and clearly expresses your perceptions.

The first thing to do in writing an observation of a child is to note physical attributes: age, sex, size, build, facial features, coloring, and so forth. However, a plain physical description gives a very static impression. For example:

> She is an Oriental girl, approximately four years of age, shorter than her peers. She has a slight build, oval face, and brown hair and eyes.

When this description of physical attributes is elaborated with some of the child's unique personal qualities: way of moving, facial expression, gestures, tone of voice, etc., the description conveys a better picture of the child as an individual different from all other individuals. The following addition conveys a much more vivid sense of the child whose physical attributes were described above.

> She had black eyebrows and lashes, brown hair, almond-shaped eyes, a fair, smooth complexion, tiny heart-shaped lips and a little pug nose. She was slim and almost fragile looking, and strolled from activity to activity with small light steps, her eyes alert and her head turning from side to side. Her arms hung slightly away from her body, swinging in rhythm to her stroll, her body swayed gracefully [Grace Kadooka, 1976].

The next step in writing the observation is to describe the

child's activities and interactions. The addition of expressive detail enhances these also.

> When she was busy doing something, she was very intent, concentrating, yet fidgeting with some part of her body. She didn't actively seek out interactions with other children but responded with a shy smile when they were initiated by someone else. She spoke little but when she did it was without hesitation [Beverly Gay, 1976].

The language used in recording is important in capturing the subtleties and complexities of children's behavior. Careful choice of words that convey the essence of the person and situation is an important part of writing vivid observations. The following examples illustrate how colorful adverbs and adjectives can enhance our ability to visualize the subject of the observation. "He had a brisk, fast pace—always rushing to where he wanted to go" (instead of "he walked faster than most children").

A good observation is specific but does not give so much detail that the point is lost. Broad general statements do not convey much information and are not very effective in capturing the important qualities of the child or interaction. For example, the statement that "John worked at stringing beads today" does not convey much specific information. We have a better picture of the child and situation when the observer tells us: "He had an intent look on his face, his tongue protruded slightly from between his teeth and it appeared that all of his concentration was focused on stringing the beads."

Additional details such as when the child worked with the beads, how long he worked, how he worked, who he worked with, and the feelings he projected as he worked might also increase the reader's ability to understand the child and the situation.

Value judgments about children should be avoided in observations unless they are clearly labeled and based on a number of observations. Describing a child as "good," "bad," "bright," "slow," "naughty," or the like, usually tells more about the values of the observer than the reality of the child. Since observations will often be communicated to children's parents and read by teachers and other professionals, teachers have the responsibility to convey useful information which is as free as possible from personal bias.

The ability to observe and to write clear and objective descriptions based on your observations is a needed skill for the teacher who must make reports on children to parents, agencies, and other teachers. This skill can be developed through practice. You can enhance your awareness and develop a greater ability to communicate by knowing about the nature of observation, by studying your writing, and by seeking feedback from others on their reactions to what you have seen and the way in which you have described it.

Kinds of Observations

The kind of observation technique you use will depend on your purpose. Observations can differ in the degree to which the process of observation and the process of recording is systematized and standardized. If your intention is to develop awareness of self or of the situation, then simply taking time to stop and observe and mentally note what is going on may be sufficient. If you are gathering information about a specific child or for a particular purpose, then some form of systematic record-keeping will be helpful. You might want to keep a pad of paper in your pocket or a central file box with a section for each child for jotting daily impressions called *anecdotal records*.

Other forms of observation may be used to collect more systematic data for diagnosis and evaluation of children.

Checklists such as those found in School Before Six: A Diagnostic Approach, the Portage Kit, and the Learning Accomplishment Profile (LAP), are very helpful tools for a teacher to use in doing systematic observations of children's development. Checklists can be used to make developmental profiles, which can provide a basis for planning activities or as a personal reference to make sure that an activity is appropriate for a particular child or group of children.

A checklist can also be used as an initial screening when you suspect that there is a problem in a child's development. While a checklist is not absolutely accurate (children vary widely and may differ in their responses from week to week), it can give an indication that you need to watch a child's development in a particular area more closely. A very general guideline is that if there is a six month developmental lag in language or a one year developmental delay in any other area, you should take it as a warning that there may be a problem and watch the child carefully. If the delay is greater than those mentioned, the child should be screened further. In many states the department of health has specialists available to do comprehensive testing and evaluation of children with developmental problems.

When observation and screening indicate that a child has a serious problem you will probably want to refer him for special help. In this case it may be necessary to write a *case study* to document the problem and your recommendations. In the case study you will summarize previous observations and perhaps include observations made by colleagues to provide other viewpoints. A case study usually includes information about the child's development, health, behavior, and family situation. It may also include samples of the child's work.

A *time-sample* is another form of a specialized observation technique which is most appropriate when a child appears to have a serious behavior problem. By recording the child's behavior at specific intervals for a period of time, teachers are able to tell if the behavior which has been concerning them occurs with sufficient frequency to constitute a problem. The time-sample technique is often used to collect baseline data to use in designing behavior modification programs for individual children. Use of a time-sample as a basis for designing a program of intervention calls for skill and may require that you study the use of the technique or seek the help of a specialist.

REFERENCES

Almy, Millie. *Ways of Studying Children.* New York: Teacher's College Press, 1959.

Blume, Susan, et al. *Portage Guide to Early Education.* Portage, Wisconsin: Cooperative Educational Service Agency, 1976.

Brophy, Jere E. ,et al. *Teaching in the Preschool.* New York: Harper and Row, 1975.

Cartwright, C., and Cartwright, P. *Developing Observation Skills.* New York: McGraw-Hill, 1974.

Cohen, Dorothy H., and Stern, Virginia. *Observing and Recording the Behavior of Young Children.* New York: Teacher's College Press, 1958.

Educational Development Center. *Exploring Childhood.* Cambridge, Mass.: EDC, 1973.

Herndon, James. *The Way it S'pozed to Be.* New York: Simon and Shuster, 1965.

Hess, Robert D., and Croft, Doreen J. *Teachers of Young Children.* Boston: Houghton Mifflin, 1972.

Hildebrand, Verna. *Introduction to Early Childhood Education,* 2nd ed. New York: Macmillan, 1976.

Hodgden, Laurel, et al. *School Before Six: A Diagnostic Approach.* St. Louis, Missouri: CEMREL Inc., 1974.

Leeper, Sarah H., et al. *Good Schools for Young Children.* New York: Macmillan, 1974.

Lindberg, Lucile, and Swerdlow, Rita. *Early Childhood Education: A Guide for Observation and Participation.* Boston: Allyn and Bacon, 1976.

Nyberg, David. *Tough and Tender Learning.* Palo Alto, Calif.: National Press Books, 1971.

Read, Katherine. *The Nursery School: A Human Relations Laboratory,* 6th ed. Philadelphia, Pa.: Saunders, 1976.

Rowen, Betty. *The Children We See: An Observational Approach to Child Study.* New York: Holt, Rinehart and Winston, 1973.

Sanford, Anne R., ed. *Learning Accomplishment Profile.* Chapel Hill, North Carolina: Training Outreach Project, Lincoln Center, 1974.

Spodek, Bernard. *Teaching in the Early Years.* Englewood Cliffs, N.J.: Prentice-Hall, 1972.

ACTIVITIES

Report on the activities assigned by:

1. Writing a 3–5 page observation paper.
2. Include in each observation:
   The day, date, and time.
   The setting.

1. Observe a child and describe:
The physical attributes of the child.
Some of the child's unique qualities.
Your interpretation of what the child may be thinking, feeling, and
   doing.
Your feelings and reactions to the child.

2. Observe an adult and a child interacting for at least ten min-
utes and describe:
The child.
The adult.
The interaction.
Your interpretation of what the child may be thinking, feeling, and
   doing.
Your interpretation of what the adult may be thinking, feeling, and
   doing.
Your feelings and reactions to the interaction.

3. Observe a child's physical development and describe:
The child.
The way the child uses his body, including

   Coordination and balance.
   Use of large muscles of the arms, legs, and body.
   Use of the small muscles of the fingers and hands.
   Coordination between eyes and hands (puzzles, bead stringing).
What inferences you can make about the child's physical develop-
   ment.
How physical development seem to influence the child's total
   functioning.
Your feelings and reactions.

4. Observe a child's social and emotional development and describe:

The child.

The child's relationship to other children.

The child's relationship to adults.

The extent to which the child is independent or dependent on others.

The extent to which the child demonstrates self-control or lack of self-control.

The child's ability to cooperate.

The primary emotion the child projects.

What inferences you can make about the child's social and emotional development.

Your feelings and reactions.

5. Observe a child's intellectual development and describe:

The child.

What knowledge and understanding about the world the child seems to have.

The child's ability to solve problems and his approach to problem-solving.

What inferences you can make about the child's intellectual development.

Your feelings and reactions.

6. If these activities do not challenge you, design your own observation with the consent of the instructor.

DISCUSSION GUIDE

1. Share with a small group of your peers a description you have written of a child. Have each person respond by sharing those words in the description that seemed strong and communicated a sense of the child to them and the words that seemed weak or vague.

2. In your small group, read a description of a child interacting with materials or a person. Have everyone write an interpretation of what the child might have been thinking, feeling, and doing. Compare to see how your interpretations were different. Check the extent to which your interpretations were based on the actual description.

3. Look at the picture of a young man interacting with children on page 130. Have each person in the small group write a brief description of what they see, their interpretation of what the adult and the children might be thinking, feeling, and doing, and their feelings and reactions to the picture. Share your observations in the group and note similarities and differences in your description, interpretation, and reactions.

4. Look at the sequence of pictures of two boys on page 131. Repeat the process you went through in the preceding activity.

5. Share in your small group anything you have learned about children and about yourself as a result of writing the observations assigned in this chapter.

RESOURCES

Almy, Millie. *Ways of Studying Children.* New York: Teacher's College Press, 1959.

Blume, Susan, et al. *Portage Guide to Early Education.* Portage: Wisconsin: Cooperative Educational Service Agency, 1976.

Cartwright, C., & Cartwright, P. *Developing Observation Skills.* New York: McGraw-Hill, 1974.

Cohen, Dorothy H., & Stern, Virginia. *Observing and Recording the Behavior of Young Children.* New York: Teacher's College Press, 1958.

Hodgden, Laurel, et al. *School Before Six: A Diagnostic Approach.* St. Louis, Missouri: CEMREL, Inc., 1974.

Lindberg, Lucile, & Swerdlow, Rita. *Early Childhood Education: A Guide for Observation and Participation.* Boston: Allyn and Bacon, 1976.

Read, Katherine. *The Nursery School: A Human Relations Laboratory,* 6th ed. Philadelphia, Pa.: Saunders, 1976.

Rowen, Betty. *The Children We See: An Observational Approach to Child Study.* New York: Holt, Rinehart & Winston, 1973.

Sanford, Anne R., ed. *Learning Accomplishment Profile.* Chapel Hill, North Carolina: Training Outreach Project, Lincoln Center, 1974.

SELF-ASSESSMENT

After you have completed the reading, activities and small-group discussions, look again at the chapter objectives. Write a short paper responding to the following questions:

1. How would you describe your awareness, knowledge, and skill regarding the subject matter of this chapter before you began reading it and doing the activities?

2. To what extent do you feel that you have achieved each of the objectives presented at the beginning of the chapter?

3. What do you see as your strengths in this area?

4. In what specific areas do you need more information and experience? What kinds?

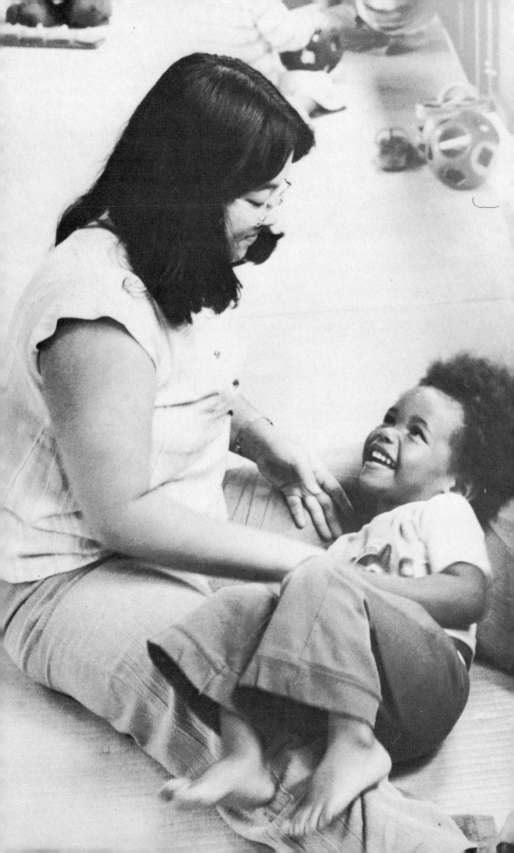

6

Interpersonal Relationships and Learning

This chapter will help you explore the role of interpersonal relationships in your work with children. In it, we introduce communication skills and management approaches that support children's development and contribute to a harmonious learning environment. Specifically, the objectives for this chapter are that you:

1. Become aware of the role of interpersonal relationships in learning.
2. Understand the ways that skill in communication helps build relationships.
3. Understand the components of effective communication.
4. Know some of the goals of classroom management.
5. Understand some management issues you will encounter as a teacher of young children and some strategies you may use.

6. Know about three theoretical approaches to classroom management and their relation to your goals for children.

7. Begin to develop skill in relating to adults and children in facilitating ways.

INTERPERSONAL RELATIONSHIPS AND LEARNING

Nothing I have ever learned of value
was taught me by an ogre. Nothing do I
regret more in my life than that
my teachers were not my friends. Nothing ever heightened
my being or deepened my learning more than being loved . . .

—J. T. Dillon
Personal Teaching, p. 153

The teacher is the single greatest factor in determining the quality of the child's school experience. Through your relationships with them children will decide if your classroom is a safe and trustworthy place in which they may live and work. And only when children feel safe, cared for and secure will they have the confidence to explore and develop new skills and understandings. In addition to determining children's feelings and attitudes toward learning, the relationships that children experience in your classroom will influence how they will relate to others.

Humanistic psychologists and educators such as Carl Rogers, Arthur Combs, and Robert Carkhuff have stressed in their writing the importance of the relationship between the teacher and the learner. They have identified interpersonal qualities such as empathy, respect, and warmth that have positive effects on the overall development of children. Research on teaching and learning supports the view of these theorists that good interpersonal relationships are of primary importance in effective teaching (Gazda, 1973, p. 9).

In this chapter we will explore two of the important ways that interpersonal relationships are expressed in the classroom: communication and classroom management.

Communication may be defined as the giving and receiving of information, signals, or messages. There are many avenues for communicating in educational settings. Teachers communicate through the environment they design for children, by their physical presence (gesture, movement, and expression), and by their words.

Communication

How the teacher communicates and what she communicates affects the degree of safety and trust the child experiences in her classroom. When a child feels threatened, anxious, or uncertain, dealing with these feelings takes energy that should be applied more profitably to using the resources available for learning. Your role as a prospective teacher is to learn to communicate in ways that help children to function both comfortably and creatively.

There are some basic communication techniques that will help you to be effective in building relationships with children. These include the ability to perceive accurately, the ability to respond authentically, sensitivity to barriers in communication, and the ability to solve interpersonal problems.

The first communication skill that you will need to develop is the ability to perceive accurately. By this we mean that you truly understand the message that another person is sending. This is very much like skill in observation in that it requires that you pay very careful attention, that you be open to the other person's communication, and that you suspend judgments and preconceived notions.

Perceiving involves more than just hearing words, because people communicate nonverbally (through facial expression, posture, and body movements) as well as verbally. Often we receive one message from a person's words while their body and expression conveys a different message.

Responding is what we do or say following another person's communication. If we wish to express caring and concern for the other person, it is important to demonstrate by our response that we really listened and understood both the words and the feelings that were conveyed.

Awareness of situational blocks to communication and of our own ineffective communication strategies are also important in achieving good communication.

Communication can be hindered by physical barriers (noise, space, temperature) and personal barriers (the physical ap-

pearance, race, or culture of the other person). Communication can also be blocked when the speaker is unaware of the effects of his communication on the other person.

Developing Communication Skills: Thomas Gordon's Framework

We have found the communication framework developed by Thomas Gordon and described in his book *Teacher Effectiveness Training* to be a very helpful guide for developing skills that are effective in working with children and adults in educational settings. Gordon assists in the acquisition of skills in hearing and accepting other people's problems, communicating your own needs and problems, and finding solutions to interpersonal problems.

Hearing and Accepting Communication about Problems. Gordon identifies four kinds of positive responses which are useful when another person has a problem which they communicate to you. These responses are called "the language of acceptance," or therapeutic communication, and consist of verbal and nonverbal behavior designed to help the other person solve his problem for himself with assistance from you.

The first is *passive listening* (silence), or listening carefully to the message being communicated without verbally responding. Listening can communicate acceptance although it may not be as effective as two-way verbal exchange.

Simple acknowledgment consists of nonverbal actions such as affirmative nods which communicate attention and acceptance.

Door openers simply put into words what is communicated nonverbally in the acknowledgment response—"Yes, I see." "Would you like to talk more about that?" These responses communicate empathy and a willingness to engage in further listening.

Active listening consists of messages which convey back to the speaker empathetic understanding of his communication.

Developing Skill in Active Listening. Gordon feels that active listening is the most useful skill that we can use when another person has a problem. The ability to really hear what a young child says is especially important because it influences whether he sees you as a person who is worthy of trust.

To understand active listening, it is useful to look at the communication process. Any message can be seen as a coded statement of the sender's internal state. What the listener hears is his own decoding of the message, as shown in the following diagram.

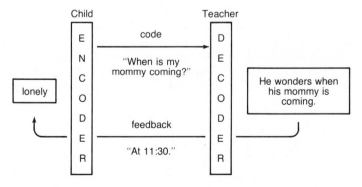

In the example given, the teacher heard the message as a neutral request for information and missed the child's strong feeling of loneliness. To engage in active listening is to listen for both the content *and* the feeling and to respond appropriately to both elements of the message. If the teacher had become aware of the child's feeling of loneliness, she might have used an active listening response which would have given the child the opportunity to examine and deal with his feelings. In that case, the previous example would look like the following:

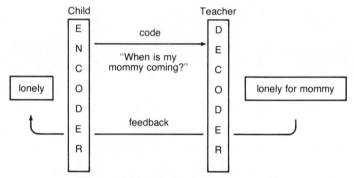

"You are anxious to see your mommy now?"

Active listening is a skill for supporting relationships through helping children (and adults) look at and deal with their own strong feelings.

When you use the active listening skill you create a safe psychological environment where people feel free to think, discuss, question, and explore because they realize that their needs will be heard and dealt with and that their feelings are acceptable.

Sometimes teacher's responses to children's communications and problems are well meaning but do not focus on the feelings and result in what Gordon calls "the language of unacceptance" or "roadblocks to communication." Some of these responses serve useful functions at the appropriate time but block communication when they are used before the communication has been really heard and understood. Our college students have found that awareness of these roadblocks and their effects is extremely useful in helping them understand the effects of their communication on others and making them more sensitive in their responses.

Listed below are the roadblocks to communication described by Gordon in *Teacher Effectiveness Training*.

TYPICAL RESPONSES TO STUDENTS' MESSAGES

1. *Ordering, Directing, Commanding* ... Telling the student to do something ... giving him an order or command.
2. *Warning, Admonishing, Threatening* ... Telling the student what consequences will occur if he does something, alluding to the use of the teacher's power.
3. *Moralizing, Preaching, Obliging* ... Telling the student what he should or ought to do.
4. *Advising, Giving Suggestions or Solutions* ... Telling the student how to solve his problem.
5. *Persuading with Logic, Arguing, Instructing, Lecturing* ... Trying to influence the student with facts, counterarguments, logic, information, or your own opinions.
6. *Judging, Criticizing, Disagreeing, Blaming* ... Making negative judgments or evaluations of a student.
7. *Praising, Agreeing, Evaluating Positively, Approving* ... Offering a positive evaluation or judgment.
8. *Name-Calling, Ridiculing, Shaming* ... Making a student feel foolish, stereotyping or categorizing him.
9. *Interpreting, Analyzing, Diagnosing* ... Telling the student what his motives are or analyzing why he is doing or saying something; communicating that you have him figured out or have him diagnosed.
10. *Reassuring, Sympathizing, Consoling, Supporting* ... Trying to make the student feel better, talking him out of his feelings, trying to make his feelings go away, denying the strength of his feelings.
11. *Probing, Questioning, Interrogating* ... Trying to find reasons, motives, causes; searching for more information to help you solve the problem.
12. *Withdrawing, Distracting, Humoring* ... Trying to get the student away from the problem, withdrawing from the problem yourself; distracting the student, kidding him out of his feelings, pushing the problem aside [Gordon, 1974, pp. 80–87].

Communicating Your Own Needs. You demonstrate acceptance of another person when he has a problem through your willingness to relate to and listen to him. When you have a problem—when your needs or your rights are being violated, Gordon recommends that you use a technique which he calls an *I-message.*

In an I-message, you take responsibility for the relationship by communicating what you are feeling without sending a message that the other person is wrong and that you don't respect or care for him. Feelings, especially unpleasant ones, are often difficult to share but it is important to avoid collecting so many negative feelings that they influence your relationships. Often teachers try so hard to be nice to children that they don't maintain their own rights in getting their needs met and respected.

When you give an I-message you can maintain your rights as a person, get your point across, and avoid hurting the other person or your relationship with him. An effective I-message has three elements:

1. A statement of the unacceptable condition or behavior.
2. A statement of the effect on you of this condition or behavior.
3. A statement of the feelings generated within you by the condition or behavior.

For example: "When you talk during story time it makes it hard for the other children to hear the story and I feel frustrated."

With such a message you do not send a negative evaluation of the child. It leaves the development of a solution to the problem the child has caused for you in the hands of the child.

A more common response to the above incident would be a message which assigns blame such as "You are a bad boy" or "You know better than to do that." A *you-message* focuses on the child's behavior in a blaming or evaluating manner. It completely ignores the issue of the affect of the behavior on you.

Solving Problems. A good learner-teacher relationship is characterized by authenticity, caring, and a commitment to work together to reach common goals. Problems do inevitably occur in the course of being together in school. In order to preserve good relationships the problems that arise should be handled immediately so that long-term resentments do not occur. Effective communication techniques can promote the solving of problems.

Gordon presents a six-step process which promotes creative solutions to mutual problems. The use of this approach often helps to prevent needless struggle and unpleasantness in handling problems. Patience and practice are needed to learn to use this technique effectively because it is a complex process and requires that you have already mastered active listening and the use of I-messages which are used at every step.

The six steps in the problem-solving process are:

1. Defining the problem in terms of what each person needs (not arguing competing solutions.)
2. Generating possible solutions (no evaluation allowed in this step.)
3. Evaluating and testing the various solutions.
4. Deciding on a mutually acceptable solution.
5. Implementing the solution.
6. Evaluating the solution.

Note. Skills in positive communication will be helpful to you as a teacher, as a parent, and as an adult relating to other adults in many settings. The books of Gordon, Ginott, Dreikurs, and others listed in the resource section of this chapter are useful for developing your awareness and skill as a communicator. Participating in class and workshop sessions where communication skills are taught and practiced and where their effective uses and abuses are discussed is another valuable way to learn to communicate and deal with problems effectively.

Classroom Management

The young child just entering school must cope with many new relationships and the demands of an entirely different physical setting. To meet these challenges and to grow in positive ways, the child needs the support of his parents and of the adults and children in the school.

As a prospective teacher, you need to be aware that children

are just beginning to learn the understandings, attitudes, and skills needed for living with groups of people and dealing with feelings. You can learn to manage a classroom in ways that promote such learning.

A central goal of classroom management is to help children learn to relate to materials, experiences, and other people in the school in harmonious ways. How you choose to achieve this goal will depend on what role you take in classroom management, the values you have for children, what you feel comfortable with, and the demands and constraints of your school setting.

Classroom management strategies can have the long-range effect of helping children feel more competent and good about themselves. Teachers who use shame and humiliation as a technique to control behavior communicate to the child that he is a bad or inadequate person.

The teacher shows respect for the child when she tells him the possible consequences of the undesirable behavior and gives him the option of controlling the behavior himself. Such an approach indicates that the child is seen as mature and intelligent enough to control his own behavior.

It is important to keep in mind the fit between what you do and what you value. Without this awareness you can accumulate a grab bag of techniques chosen because they appear to be effective. Your decisions about the success of management techniques should focus on whether the outcome was consistent with your long-range goals for the children's development rather than on whether the technique worked at a particular moment.

You will need to learn to deal with three basic issues in classroom management:

1. How to interact with children to help them handle their feelings and problems in constructive ways.
2. How to develop rules which minimize problems and conflicts.
3. How to handle the conflicts which do occur.

In the following sections we discuss some ways you might address each of these issues.

Helping Children Handle Feelings and Problems

A child enters a classroom setting with his whole self—needs, developmental stage, established likes and dislikes, communication style, behavior patterns, and his unique perception of the world. Some of these things may bring him into conflict in a school setting. When you meet a child, you need to respect him and accept all of his characteristics if his potential is to be realized.

You can help a child understand the effects of his behavior patterns on himself, on others, and on the total functioning of the school environment. When he enters your school, the child needs to learn many things—what behaviors work in the new setting, how to handle routines and materials, how space is used, how you expect him to behave. Frequently, his conflicts in the new setting result because he lacks information. You will need to communicate your expectations with clarity and

simplicity and repeat them as many times as the child may need to learn what you consider appropriate in your setting.

In addition to helping children learn expectations, you can provide alternatives to nonproductive or disruptive behavior. This is especially true if you expect a child to give up a behavior he has found useful in other settings or one he uses to meet some basic emotional need. The child may need a long time and a lot of courage to change from an old reliable behavior to a new untested behavior, even when the old one is no longer working for him.

One way you can help children learn to control disruptive behavior is by personally using problem-solving techniques rather than retaliative words and actions to deal with your feelings of anger and frustration, and by helping them experience how much more useful such techniques are in making relationships work. Children can learn that behavior that hurts people or destroys things is not a productive way to handle problems in a group. With practice, they can learn to tell each other how they feel and what they want instead of striking out when a confrontation occurs.

Another way you can help is to be aware when children seem about to come into conflict and intervene to help them find constructive alternatives. When a child has participated in finding the solution to a problem, he is much more likely to put the solution into action. He also gains a sense that it is possible to successfully search for alternatives and may try that approach in future conflicts.

Here are some examples of teacher communications that help children learn constructive ways of dealing with problems:

"You don't need to hit Josh to get your truck back. Tell him what you need."

"I won't let you hurt Sherry! You can tell her that what she did made you feel angry."

"Can you think of another way to solve your problem?"

"I see you're upset about what happened. How can you let him know?"

Following are some suggestions for classroom management.

SUGGESTIONS FOR CLASSROOM MANAGEMENT

- As the noise level rises, talk softer. Usually the children will listen out of curiosity.
- To get the attention of an offending child, move close (on his level) and speak directly to him.
- Use children's names in positive situations instead of only when correcting behavior or scolding. Use names to approve an action, to offer assistance, and in conversation so that children don't get the message that you only notice them when they are disruptive.
- Use positive rather than negative language in correcting behavior.

For ...	Substitute ...
"Don't run with the scissors."	"Scissors need to stay on the table so no one will get hurt by them."
"Don't get your clothes dirty."	"You need a smock for painting."
"Don't tear the book."	"Turn the pages carefully."

- Creating competition between children can be damaging to self-esteem. It is best to avoid phrases like "George is going to be the first one through"; "I really like how quietly Susie is listening"; "Look at how fast Jim is running."
- Offer choices only when you intend that the child make a choice. "Would you give me the knife?" is not appropriate when you mean "I must have the knife right now; it is dangerous!"

> • Saying that "big children don't" or that they are "acting like babies" is destructive to self-esteem.
> • Listen to children and find ways to respond to what they have to say in constructive ways.

Rules

A rule is a guide or regulation for action. In a school, rules function to enable people to work together in harmony.

Clear guidelines for behavior are essential in making a program for children function effectively. Two types of problems regarding rules occur frequently in early childhood programs. Some programs have so many rules and requirements for behavior that it is difficult to remember them. In these programs teachers either spend most of their time enforcing rules or enforce them sporadically and without clarity about which rules are necessary. In other programs teachers don't want to impinge on children's freedom and spontaneity and, consequently, tend to have too few rules to protect children's safety and the orderliness of the learning environment.

Care should be taken to establish only those rules which are necessary in making the setting function for children and adults. Children accept and abide by rules that are reasonable, clearly stated, and consistently enforced. The number of rules should be kept to a minimum and should require behavior appropriate for the developmental level of the children. For example, it is unreasonable to make rules requiring young children to sit quietly for long periods of time. Children respect rules when they understand the reason for them and when they have a part in determining them.

Following are some examples of rules and their reasons:

Rule	*Reason*
We do not disturb other people's work.	If we run and shout it is hard for other people to do their work.
We do not hit people.	We don't hit people be-

	cause it is painful and no one likes to be hurt.
Toys and games stay in the classroom.	If Tinker Toys go outside the pieces can get lost and then we won't have them to use.
We put away materials after use.	Everyone needs to clean-up after activities so the school will be clean and orderly for us to use.

Conflict Management

Even in the best-designed settings, young children sometimes come into conflict with other children and adults in the course of the normal daily interaction in the classroom. Often one or more of the children in the classroom have personal problems and previous patterns of interaction which involve them in frequent and severe conflict; others resort to lashing out when they are tired, frustrated, or lack strategies for handling a problem.

You as a teacher can help children develop successful strategies for handling strong feelings and conflicts by becoming sensitive to the inner feelings and struggles that bring a child into confrontation with others. You can acknowledge children's strong feelings and encourage them to talk about these feelings and to develop alternative behaviors. Children need to learn that it is all right to have strong feelings and to express them, but that they must not act on these feelings in ways that hurt people or property.

We have found the approach used by Bruno Bettelheim in his book *Love is Not Enough* (1950) extremely effective as a guideline for handling destructive behavior and for reassuring violent children who usually fear retaliation. Bettelheim tells a destructive child that he will not allow the child to hurt himself or hurt another person, nor will he let anyone else cause injury to the child. As children learn that their feelings will be respected and their needs met and that others will not be allowed to hurt them, they usually turn less and less to destructive behavior. Corporal punishment is not appropriate in an early childhood program. Children who have been harshly punished behave appropriately when there is threat of punishment but may, at a later time, tend to show increased aggressive behavior.

Acknowledging acceptable behavior and communicating clearly that a behavior is unacceptable seems to us to be effective and more consistent with the goal of aiding the child to develop self-control and a positive view of himself. Following are some suggestions for managing conflict:

SUGGESTIONS FOR MANAGING CONFLICT

- When a child is lashing out violently, act immediately to protect persons and property.
- It is important to be aware when talk is no longer affecting behavior and it is time to enact consequences.
- A time-out technique where a child is sent out of the situation for a predetermined period of time is often useful for calming him and letting him think about more constructive ways to behave (provided it is not initiated in a punitive manner).
- Communicate your dislike of destructive behavior while demonstrating a basic caring for the child.
- It is more useful to engage a child in finding *what* can be done to prevent something from occurring again than to try to find out *who* was to blame or *why* something happened.
- Harsh punishment or rough handling frightens children and often results in their treating their peers in a similar way.
- In a violent outburst it is often effective to hold the child firmly in your arms to restrain and calm him and to communicate your caring.

Conflict is inevitable in life and in the classroom. The way you deal with conflict is an important model for young children. Their experience can be that conflict is violently disruptive and is harshly controlled or they can see conflict as natural part of life and as an opportunity for problem-solving.

Management Approaches
There are a number of approaches which have been designed to give guidance to teachers and parents in the theory and practice of child management. These approaches differ in underlying philosophy and techniques, and reflect a variety of values. We will discuss three of these theoretical approaches as they have been applied to classroom management; the humanistic approach based on the work of Carl Rogers, the democratic approach based on the work of Alfred Adler, and the behaviorist approach based on the work of B. F. Skinner.

In the humanistic approach the values of positive self-regard and individual responsibility for the direction of one's life are emphasized. In the democratic approach the individual's ability to function cooperatively in social settings is valued. The behaviorist approach stresses the creation of a purposeful and orderly learning environment through the shaping of children's behavior in desired directions. Though they reflect different values, all three approaches offer valuable techniques for teachers when applied thoughtfully in the service of the development of the whole child.

The Humanistic Approach

The humanistic philosophy and therapeutic practices of Rogers have been applied to classroom management practices by a number of interpreters including Thomas Gordon and Haim Ginott.

In a humanistic approach to classroom management the teacher's central task is to humanize relationships between individuals and within groups and to help children develop their unique potential and capacity to see the world and themselves positively. To accomplish these goals the teacher needs skills for achieving open, honest, and authentic communication. These skills include active listening, sending nonjudgmental messages about the effects of behavior, and problem-solving in an open-ended manner without needing control over the outcomes. In addition, the teacher must be willing to change her own behavior as part of a mutually satisfactory solution. Development of these basic skills in relating to children are described in the preceding sections of this chapter.

Insight and skill in the application of humanistic principles in classrooms can be gained from the writing of Gordon in *Teacher Effectiveness Training* and Ginott in *Teacher and Child*. These give many practical suggestions for relating to children in educational settings.

The Democratic Approach

Rudolf Dreikurs has interpreted and applied to classroom management practice many of the ideas of Adler's Individual Psychology. In Dreikur's democratic approach to classroom management the child is viewed as a social being with a strong desire to be part of a group. A child's disruptive behavior is seen as a result of his inability to be part of the group in a positive and cooperative manner. When the child feels unsuccessful in gaining acceptance within the group he becomes discouraged and tries to gain entrance in disruptive ways.

The teacher's central task in this approach is to help the child discover his mistaken ways of gaining group approval and help him become a respectful and responsible member of a democratic group of his peers. The teacher does this by establishing a model group in which the child learns the laws of living as a member of society through confronting the direct consequences of his behavior. The teacher functions as the group leader and employs the democratic concepts of respect, cooperation and participation in decision-making.

Psychology in the Classroom and other books by Dreikurs contain many suggestions for how teachers can lead classroom groups toward a democratic social climate.

The Behaviorist Approach

The behavior management principles and techniques developed by Skinner have been interpreted and applied to classroom management practices by many learning theorists and educators. Behaviorists see misbehavior as a function of mislearning—being rewarded for the wrong behaviors.

Behaviorists believe that all behavior is a function of external stimuli and that procedures for evoking desired behavior and changing undesired behavior can be taught. When used in classrooms behaviorist procedures allow the teacher to respond to children and control events so that the child behaves according to the prescriptions of the adult. The adult does not engage in conflict. He decides which behavior is to be established or extinguished.

We have found Lilian Katz's paper "Condition with Caution" (Katz, 1971) a useful reminder that behaviorist techniques are only appropriate when the child's negative behavior is an outcome of his conditioning. Other approaches are called for when disruptive behavior is caused by lack of information about appropriate behavior or emotional problems.

Selecting Management Strategies

All of these approaches can be used in ways that take into account individual needs and which show respect and caring for children. Techniques can be chosen which fit a particular situation and your personal philosophy and developmental goals for children.

The communication and problem-solving skills presented in humanistic approaches are helpful for building relationships and dealing with everyday upsets and problems. When conficts arise the democratic approach is helpful for understanding the mistaken strategies that children have adopted and for helping them to redirect their behavior more positively. And when destructive patterns have developed and become habitual the consistency and power of reinforcement techniques may be effective in changing or eliminating the behaviors.

REFERENCES

Bettelheim, Bruno. *Love is Not Enough.* New York: Free Press, 1950.

Carkhuff, Robert R. *The Art of Helping.* Amherst: Human Resources Development, 1972.

Combs, Arthur W.; Richards, Anne Cohen; & Richards, Fred. *Perceptual Psychology.* New York: Harper and Row, 1976.

Dillon, J. T. *Personal Teaching.* Columbus, Ohio: Charles E. Merrill Publishing Co., 1971.

Dreikurs, Rudolf. *Psychology in the Classroom.* New York: Harper and Row, 1968.

Erikson, Erik H. *Childhood and Society.* New York: Norton, 1963.

Fargo, Jean M. *Education for Parenthood in the Community College.* University of Washington. Unpublished Doctoral Dissertation, 1974.

Gazda, George M. *Human Relations Development.* Boston: Allyn and Bacon, 1975.

Ginott, Haim. *Teacher and Child.* New York: Macmillan, 1972.

Glasser, William. *Schools Without Failure.* New York: Harper and Row, 1961.

Gordon, Thomas. *Teacher Effectiveness Training.* New York: Peter H. Wyden, 1974.

Katz, Lilian G. "Condition with Caution: Think Thrice Before Conditioning." *Preschool Education Newsletter,* February 1971.

Maslow, Abraham. *Toward a Psychology of Being.* New York: Van Nostrand Reinhold, 1968.

Read, Katherine. *The Nursery School: A Human Relations Laboratory,* 6th ed. Philadelphia: Saunders, 1976.

Rogers, Carl. *Freedom to Learn.* Columbus, Ohio: Charles E. Merrill, 1969.

ACTIVITIES

Report on the activities assigned by:

1. Writing a 3–5 page reaction paper or making a cassette tape.
2. Using another medium (tape, photography, drawing, etc.) with the consent of the instructor.

1. Observe a teacher interacting with children. What do you notice about: the way she listens to children, the way she responds to children, the relationships between verbal and nonverbal behavior? What do you feel she is communicating to the children? What are your reactions to her communication style?

2. On a cassette tape, make a 10–15 minute recording in which you engage with a child in dialogue. Analyze your dialogue, using basic concepts from Gordon's communication framework. Did you actively listen? Did you give any roadblocks? Did you use I-messages? What did you notice about your style of communication?

3. Observe a teacher interacting with children and notice the ways in which she responds to children's feelings and problems. Evaluate her responses in terms of how they help the children understand problems and feelings. Do her responses help children find constructive solutions to problems?

4. Observe the rules in a classroom by watching the teacher, listening to what she says about rules and other evidence (rules listed, or reported by children). Evaluate how effective the rules are in supporting the functioning of children and teachers in the classroom. What do the rules suggest about what the teacher values for children?

5. Observe a teacher handling a conflict in a classroom. Describe the conflict and her method of dealing with it. Evaluate the teacher's effectiveness in handling the conflict. How do you think the children felt? What were your reactions to the interaction?

6. Collect at least ten samples of management interactions in a classroom. Include what the child did and how the teacher responded. Analyze each interaction in terms of the immediate and possible long-term effects. How effective was each management technique? How do you think the child felt in each case?

7. Describe a situation in which you handled a conflict between two children or between you and a child. What techniques did you use? How effective was your handling of the situation? How did you feel? How do you think the child felt? If you could do it again what might you do differently and why?

8. If these activities do not challenge you, design your own activity with the consent of the instructor.

DISCUSSION GUIDE

1.   Recall a relationship you had with a teacher as a young child in school. What can you remember about communication and learning in her classroom?

2.   Recall an incident in which you were punished or reprimanded at school. What happened? How did you feel?

3.   What do you think were the major goals of the rules and management techniques you experienced at school? At home? How effective were they in accomplishing these goals?

4.   Choose a teacher you have recently observed and describe the kind of communication she has with children. How effective is she in communicating with children? What are your reactions to her style of communication?

5.   Describe some of the rules and management techniques you have observed in a classroom setting. Evaluate the effectiveness of these rules and techniques. How do you imagine children feel about these rules and management techniques?

6.   What other criteria can be used to evaluate a classroom management technique besides "It works"?

RESOURCES

Bettelheim, Bruno. *Love is Not Enough.* New York: Free Press, 1950.

Gazda, George. *Human Relations Development.* Boston: Allyn and Bacon, 1975.

Glasser, William. *Schools Without Failure.* New York: Harper and Row, 1961.

Katz, Lilian. "Condition With Caution: Think Thrice Before Conditioning." *Preschool Education Newsletter,* February 1971.

Maslow, Abraham. *Toward a Psychology of Being.* New York: Van Nostrand Reinhold, 1968.

Read, Katherine. *The Nursery School: Human Relationships and Learning,* 6th ed. Philadelphia: Saunders, 1976.

Behaviorist

Krumboltz, John D., & Krumboltz, Helen B. *Changing Children's Behavior.* Englewood Cliffs, N.J.: Prentice-Hall, 1972.

Patterson, Gerald R., & Gullian, M. Elizabeth. *Living with Children. New Methods for Parents and Teachers,* revised ed. Champaign, Ill.: Research Press Co., 1971.

Democratic

Dinkmeyer, D., & Dreikurs, R. *Encouraging Children to Learn, The Encouragement Process.* New Hampshire: Prentice-Hall, 1963.

Dreikurs, R., & Slotz, V. *Children: The Challenge.* New York: Hawthorn Books, 1964.

Dreikurs, R., & Grey, L. *Logical Consequences: A New Approach to Discipline.* New York: Meredith, 1968.

Dreikurs, Rudolf. *Psychology in the Classroom.* New York: Harper and Row, 1968.

Humanistic

Ginott, Haim. *Teacher and Child.* New York: Macmillan, 1972.

Gordon, Thomas. *Teacher Effectiveness Training.* New York: Peter H. Wyden, 1974.

Rogers, Carl. *Client-Centered Therapy.* Boston: Houghton Mifflin, 1965.

Satir, Virginia. *Peoplemaking.* Palo Alto, Calif.: Science & Behavior Books, 1972.

SELF-ASSESSMENT

After you have completed the reading, activities, and small-group discussions, look again at the chapter objectives. Write a short paper responding to the following questions.

1. How would you describe your awareness, knowledge, and skill regarding the subject matter of this chapter before you began reading it and doing the activities?

2. To what extent do you feel that you have achieved each of the objectives presented at the beginning of the chapter?

3. What do you see as your strengths in this area?

4. In what specific areas do you need more information and experience? What kinds?

7

The Learning Environment

This chapter will help you to organize space, provide equipment and materials, and plan the use of time to support the growth and development of young children. Specifically, the objectives for this chapter are that you:

1. Understand how the environment can communicate to children that you care about them.
2. Develop skill in designing physical settings that meet children's basic needs.
3. Understand how the arrangement of indoor and outdoor space affects the way children function in the environment.
4. Develop skill in organizing indoor and outdoor space which reflects your goals for children.
5. Understand how equipment and materials contribute to children's development.

177

6. Develop skill in choosing and arranging equipment and materials to support your developmental goals for children.

7. Understand how scheduling of activities affects how children function in the classroom.

8. Develop skill in evaluating the way time is used in classrooms and in developing routines and schedules which promote the achievement of your goals for children.

THE LEARNING ENVIRONMENT

The child's physical environment speaks to him. When he enters your classroom and he can tell if it is a place intended for him and how you want him to use it. A cozy corner with a rug, cushions, and books suggests "Sit here and look at books." A ladder supported by two saw horses and connected to the ground by a plank says "Climb up, go across any way you can think of, jump down."

An airy environment with light, color, warmth, and interesting materials to be explored sends a clear message: "We care—this is a place for children." In such settings, there is enough space to move comfortably, the furnishings are child-size, and the arrangement suggests how materials can be used.

In this chapter, we help you learn how to design a learning environment that meets the needs of children and supports your values and developmental goals.

As a teacher, you will have to make choices in designing your classroom which will directly affect the quality of both the child's relationship to people and to learning materials. In making these choices, you need to look at three very basic questions:

1. Is the environment appropriate for the developmental stage of the children?

2. How does the environment affect human relationships (between children, between children and adults, and between adults)?

3. How does the environment facilitate children's learning?

In the following sections we explore three broad components of the learning environment—space, equipment and materials, and time. These are presented in an order which may be useful in designing a program. First, you consider how you might use the physical space. Then you determine what materials and equipment are needed and how they might best be arranged and stored. Finally, you plan the way time will be scheduled throughout the day.

Space

In this section, we look at how to create an environment in which children's basic needs for safety and comfort are met and in which children and adults can live and work together. Then we discuss how to organize space to support learning.

Safe Space

Safe space has two dimensions—psychological and physical. Psychological safety involves the child's perceptions. A child can tell when and where he is welcome. A child knows he is in a safe, trustworthy place if his needs are cared for, if people show their respect in the ways they listen and talk to him, and if the space arrangement is orderly, comfortable, and attractive.

It is important that the environment be safe physically as well as psychologically. The teacher needs to be aware of the hazards in the setting and be prepared to deal with inevitable emergency situations.

Being aware of safety includes being certain of the basic soundness and good repair of the building, equipment, and materials; protecting children from dangerous substances; and avoiding hazards like exposed outlets or electric cords in pathways. Preparedness involves anticipating dangerous situations such as fire or accidents, planning how to deal with emergencies, having training in basic first-aid procedures, and having first-aid supplies available in the school.

It is important to remain attentive to safety requirements, not only as you design the school environment but in everyday

practice. You need to give children the safety information they need in new situations such as field trips and in the introduction of new equipment or unfamiliar materials. You can further insure the children's well-being by helping them to recognize hazards and activities that may be dangerous and by teaching them procedures for handling emergencies. It will help children to understand and cooperate in safety procedures if you communicate the rationale for your concerns.

Structuring Space for Learning

When the child knows that you and the environment are trustworthy, he can direct his energy to exploring and experimenting in a setting designed to help him learn and grow. The amount of choice the child has in the use of space has important implications for the way the program is organized and the kind of learning which occurs.

The use of space in a classroom can be looked at as a continuum. One end of the continuum represents an arrangement of space which allows activities to occur simultaneously with maximum child choice. The informal class with individual, small group, or quiet and noisy activities happening at the same time illustrates such a setting. This use of space is appropriate in programs which view children as capable of making wise choices when given an array of activities in a classroom structured for independent learning.

The other end of the continuum represents an arrangement in which the entire space must be used in the same way at the same time. A traditional classroom with bolted down desks is an example of such a setting. This use of space is suitable in traditional academic programs in which the adult directs all of the learning.

Usually space organization in an early childhood program will fall somewhere between these extremes. The way you choose to organize space for learning will depend on your values, your goals for children, staffing patterns, and resources available. If you wish to emphasize the process of learning and trust that children will choose what they need, you will provide an environment which is rich in materials and which allows children many choices. If you are concerned with the acquisition of specific skills or understandings, you may choose to structure space to minimize distractions so that children can focus on specific instructional tasks.

Arrangement of Indoor Space. Most preschools and many kindergartens and primary classrooms organize space into areas for art, science, blocks, books, dramatic play, music, woodworking, and manipulative toys and games—which early childhood educators regard as developmentally appropriate learning experiences for young children.

When you begin to design a classroom, it is a good idea to begin by defining specific areas for different types of activities—messy, active, quiet, small group, large group. Art and block areas can be located first since each has its particular requirements. The art area should be near the water and requires a washable floor; the block area should be large, carpeted if possible to reduce noise, and set away from traffic. Other areas can be fitted into the remaining space, keeping in mind that each should be organized so that adults can observe children's interactions with each other and with materials and to facilitate supervision of the entire classroom.

Independence and exploration are fostered by arrangements which allow children to choose activities, to find materials and put them away, and to move easily from one activity to another.

Wise arrangement of space can prevent disruption of activities either from adjacent areas or by children's movement from one activity to another. To reduce disturbance, clear unobstructed pathways should be created between areas and noisy activities should be separated from quieter ones.

Space arrangement can communicate clearly to children what it is possible to do in each area and what the expectations are. Dead space (large areas with no obvious boundaries or unobstructed pathways from door to door) encourage children to run and wrestle and should be avoided if you wish to control these behaviors indoors.

Arrangement of Outdoor Space. Outdoor space can be as stimulating as indoor space. Outdoor spaces can be used for an endless variety of learning activities. Animals, gardens, sandboxes, and water play located outdoors can be the source for science, math, language development, and creative activities. Messy materials like clay and paint are especially well suited to outdoor use.

Typically in the early childhood program, the outdoor area is used as a site for apparatus for physical development. Playground equipment and play structures are a very important component of the outdoor environment and should be designed thoughtfully with developmental goals in mind.

Constructing a play yard from improvised materials may have advantages. Tires, wood planks, crates, and cartons can be found or purchased inexpensively. Homemade equipment lends itself to flexible use and offers variety to the children, especially if they have a part in designing it.

When outdoor space is not available for active play due to climate, it is important to provide children with opportunities for vigorous indoor activity such as creative movement or tumbling.

Equipment and Materials

Good equipment and materials are essential in an early childhood program for they suggest directions and provide the raw materials for children's exploration and learning.

Through interaction with well-designed equipment and materials, children develop large- and small-muscle coordination, intelligence, creativity, social skills, and self-awareness. Good equipment and materials can do much to facilitate growth in all of these areas of development.

Generally, the term *equipment* refers to furniture and other large and expensive items in the school, such as easels, climbing apparatus, dramatic play area furnishings. *Material* refers to smaller and less expensive items in the school, such as puzzles, games, books, and toys and also to items like paint, felt pens, glue, and paper, which are replaced regularly.

Any item that a teacher brings into a learning environment for children should be chosen carefully. There are a number of criteria that will help in selecting items that will serve children well. Good equipment and materials are attractive, feel good to touch and hold, are well-constructed, work properly, fit children's abilities and interests, and can be used by children of different ages.

Many good materials for young children can be used in a variety of ways (for example, sand can be used for pouring, building, sensory exploration, dramatic play, etc.). A program for young children may contain natural materials like earth, sand, water, and clay; manufactured materials; and materials designed and made by teachers. It will have materials which can be used in many ways (paint, paper) as well as those that have one prescribed use (puzzles, hammers, etc.).

Selecting Equipment and Materials for Learning

In this section we describe basic equipment and materials, consider how they can be arranged and used, and how they contribute to children's development. A program that strives to provide an environment that supports the development of young children will have a number of different types of materials and equipment:

> natural play materials
>
> equipment for active play
>
> construction toys
>
> manipulative toys

materials for dramatic play

art materials

books

cognitive materials

Natural Materials. Through play with natural materials such as sand, clay, and water, children learn mathematical concepts like volume and measurement. They learn about the properties of substances through pouring, feeling, and mixing. Sandboxes and water-play areas are often found outdoors; they can also be located indoors where climate and space so dictate.

Woodworking helps children develop coordination and skill in using tools and offers many challenges in measurement and construction. Children need tools that are sturdy and in working order. The smallest-scale adult tools provide the best woodworking experiences for young children. Woodworking needs to be carefully supervised.

Active Play Equipment. Equipment for active play offers opportunity for vigorous movement and exploration. Active play helps a child develop and explore his physical limits and learn many spatial concepts (up, down, under, over) by experiencing them with his own body.

Simple, inexpensive equipment such as sturdy wooden boxes, planks, tires, cardboard cartons, as well as such structures provided by nature as logs and trees, can encourage active play. Swings, slides, seesaws, and rocking toys, tricycles, and bicycles offer opportunities to use and develop the large muscles of the arms and legs and provide experience in balance and coordination.

Construction Materials. Construction toys like blocks, Lego, and Tinker Toys provide learning experiences in measurement, ratio, and problem-solving and help children learn to work together.

A full set of hardwood unit-sized blocks is an invaluable part of a learning environment for young children. Unit blocks demonstrate mathematical relationships to the child when he discovers that two blocks of one size equal one larger block. Block play can be enhanced and extended through the addition of toy cars, trucks, and representations of animal and human figures.

Manipulative Materials. Manipulative materials like puzzles, beads, pegboards, and lotto games are designed to give children practice in hand-eye coordination and the development of the small muscles of their fingers and hands. These experiences are important preparation for writing and expose children to concepts like color, size, and shape, which help in developing the ability to recognize letters and words.

Dramatic Play Materials. Dramatic play materials provide learning experiences and practice in the skills of daily living—both in the manipulation of the physical equipment and management of the relationships. Children imitate the actions of the very important grown-ups in their lives and thus learn about how the various adult roles might feel.

Materials for dramatic play can be organized in a play area which may include dolls, dress-up clothes (for boys as well as girls), common objects from daily life such as pots, pans, brooms, and mops (child-size). Often the area is organized into a housekeeping area which emphasizes domestic activity but it can present other themes—post office, hospital, or store. We know one teacher who, when she found the boys staying away from the housekeeping area, converted it to a ranch-style bunk house.

Art Materials. Art materials provide opportunities for creative expression and physical development. It is important that a range of media be available. A good selection of art materials includes paint, clay, and play dough, collage materials, and materials for three-dimensional construction.

Books. The best way to help children learn the joy of reading and become motivated to read is to have good books available and use them often. Children need many opportunities to look at books, to hear stories, and to see adults using and enjoying books. The use of books is encouraged when you provide a library area that is comfortable, quiet, and well-stocked with a selection of developmentally appropriate, good quality children's books. The books can be displayed on shelves at the children's eye level and accompanied with attractive displays of related projects and children's art.

Cognitive Materials. All of the types of materials and equipment described in this section contribute to the in-

tellectual development of children. Activities such as woodworking, cooking, and block building are especially important
in helping children develop mathematics and science concepts.
In addition, materials such as rulers, scales, balances, lotto,
and matching games often found in math and science learning
centers build concepts about the world through the processes
of comparison, classification, and measurement.

Arrangement and Storage

If you wish to encourage children to develop independence and
responsibility, materials should be well-organized and stored
in open areas at the children's eye level. Cartons, or containers
with labels or pictures which indicate the contents, help children keep materials in good condition and return them to the
same place. If open shelves are used, storing materials in containers or dividing the shelf with a strip of colored tape will
help differentiate areas. Storage areas which contain materials
used primarily by the teachers need to be clearly indicated so

that children can tell which areas are for them and which are not. It is important that all new materials be introduced to children and the proper ways of using, storing, and caring for them discussed. This may be time consuming in the beginning, but saves time in the long run.

Time In this section we examine how to establish routines which meet children's needs and then discuss how to schedule time to promote learning.

Routines

Routines are the regular, more or less unvarying procedures of school life. The teacher provides routines to enable the children to use the school environment during the course of the day to meet their personal needs. Some important routines each day are arrival, cleanup, rest time, toileting, and mealtime.

When daily routines are predictable, children know what to expect next and are not left in confusion without resources for ordering and understanding their experiences. The trust created by routines that are both nurturing and predictable frees the child to develop relationships with others and grow and learn.

Children feel comfortable in their setting when they see that the routines are reasonable and purposeful. If you communicate your good reasons for establishing a routine and your commitment to having it work, children's resistance to routines can be reduced. Here are some guidelines we have found useful for dealing with the following regular, daily routines: arrival, cleanup, rest time, toileting, and mealtime.

Arrival at school each day can be a friendly and relaxed time for the child. Even though the initial adjustment to school has been made, the young child may find disturbing the transition from the familiar care of his family to the more recently developed school relationships.

An arrival period during which the teacher is free to personally greet and talk briefly with every parent and child as they enter school sets a relaxed tone. At this time the teacher can notice if each child is in good health and ready to be in school.

Cleanup procedures prepare an area for the next activity and keep the classroom functional. You may say to a child, "It is time to clean up the room so we can have a pleasant place to eat lunch." Children can understand that they are members of a community and that they need to share in the responsibility for keeping it clean and orderly.

Rest time need not be a difficult time for children and teachers. Teachers can reduce problems by sharing the reasons for rest time so that children understand the importance of relaxing their minds and bodies. Children may resist resting if others are still doing interesting things or if they are required to rest when they are not yet tired. If you do not insist that children sleep but rather let them use rest time as a period for quiet relaxation they may respond more positively.

Toileting: Children are often anxious and reluctant about using the toilet facilities in the school. They will become comfortable with the facilities and procedures if you are patient and help them learn what is expected of them. Scolding, shaming, or punishing toilet accidents result in fear, resentment, and increased anxiety.

Children can be helped to be self-reliant in toileting if the toilet facilities are child-size and accessible to them. It is not appropriate to have a set schedule for toilet use because very young children cannot regulate their bodies by a clock.

Mealtime can be pleasant when it is orderly enough to focus on eating and casual enough to be a social experience. Some of the nicest moments of the day occur when teachers and children have a chance to converse during their snack or lunch.

Resistance and fears around eating are common. Concern should be focused on communicating to children that you will neither force them to eat or deny them the opportunity to eat for any reason.

Young children become restless and irritable when they are expected to wait until everyone is served, to wait while others finish, or to hurry because others are waiting. Many problems can be avoided if you have a set procedure for dismissing children who have finished eating (for example, allowing children to leave the table to read a book or to play quietly with a game or toy).

Structuring the Day

Once routines have been established, you can focus on scheduling activities that promote children's development. The use of time in a classroom can be thought of as existing on a continuum, one end representing child-chosen use of time and the other, teacher-chosen use of time.

Most programs seek a balance between child- and teacher-chosen use of time that reflects their goals and philosophy. Most often the broad time frame is established by teachers and during activity periods (which can range in length from one half-hour to two hours) children are free to choose the specific areas and activities they want to engage in.

In programs which emphasize process, children make many decisions about how to use their time. The schedule can be organized around fixed points in the day: arrival, snack, lunch, nap, and departure, with several long activity periods during which children choose what they will do. Teachers in this type of program need to put great care and effort into designing learning areas so the environment suggests possible uses of and encourages interactions with materials. In some programs children have a great deal of choice in how to use space as well as how to use time. In these settings the children choose whether they want to engage in indoor or outdoor activities and may move freely between these areas.

In programs characterized by a greater focus on content, time is usually divided into small units, with parts of the day regularly reserved for activities such as art, music, story, snack, specific learning tasks, and outdoor time.

Group Activities. Group activities which require every child's attention should be kept to a minimum and carefully planned since young children vary in interest and attention span. Children enjoy one or two scheduled group periods a day for an activity such as music, story time, or teacher-directed learning tasks. Other times for coming together as a group are snack and lunch time. The length of a scheduled group session should depend on the activity, mood, and developmental stage of the children, and the personal style, skill, and educational objectives of the teacher.

During a group activity, children need to be free to wiggle and move their bodies. Often this can be built into the activity. Story time can be broken up with finger plays which let the children stand and stretch. During the music or movement time, activities which require movement can be interspersed with sitting activities.

Some things are very difficult to do with large groups of children, for example, cooking, lively group discussions, and games in which children must take turns. These activities are most worthwhile when you can work with just a few children at a time. If the adult-child ratio in a school doesn't allow the luxury of small groups, special care must be put into designing the activities so they will hold the attention of the children. Since it can be difficult to keep the undivided attention of a large group of young children, many teachers have found that it works best to allow children who have trouble participating to observe or choose a quiet activity during a group activity.

Transition Times

Each time an activity period is ended, there is a transition—a time of gathering the children together or movement into a new activity. Transition times can be made smoothly and in a relaxed manner with planning and preparation. Children adjust to changes in activities if the major activities of the day regularly follow one another.

It is helpful to give children who are absorbed in an activity several minutes warning before the actual transition begins. You can help a child who is not finished by suggesting a time later in the day or the next day when he can complete a project. A child wishing to begin a project near a transition needs to be warned that he doesn't have much time.

Children who are waiting for the next activity to begin are unlikely to do so silently. You can sit with a waiting group and sing and talk with them while another person helps the remainder finish up. You might start story time with a finger play or a song while waiting for the group to gather or have the children look at books or listen to music.

You can avoid a great stampede or excessive regimentation by dismissing a few children at a time in a manner that suits the new activity. For example, if children are moving from a large group activity to interest centers in the classroom, you might dismiss them individually or in groups of two or three. Techniques for dismissal can include the use of chants or songs which include the child's name and what he may do next, such as, "J-O-H-N go wash your hands and get your lunch." Another technique is to use some attribute which children can recognize as the basis for dismissal: "Everyone with the color red on their shirt may go to the play area."

Experienced teachers design many creative ways for making transitions smooth and comfortable. You may wish to collect such ideas or invent your own.

REFERENCES

Feeney, Stephanie, & Marion Magarick. "Good Toys for Young Children," Sound Filmstrip and Guide. Honolulu, Hawaii: Curriculum Research and Development Group, University of Hawaii, 1976.

Harms, Thelma. "Evaluating Settings for Learning," in Katherine Baker Read (Ed.), *Ideas That Work with Young Children.* Washington, D.C.: NAEYC, 1972.

Headstart Regional Training Office. "Space for Learning." Washington, D.C.: Department of Health, Education, and Welfare, 1972.

Kritchevsky, Sybil, & Elizabeth Prescott, with Lee Walling. *Physi-*

cal *Space: Planning Environments for Young Children.* Washington, D.C.: NAEYC, 1969.

Prescott, Elizabeth. "Approaches to Quality in Early Childhood Programs." *Childhood Education,* 1974, *50,* 125–131.

Read, Katherine B. *The Nursery School: Human Relationships and Learning,* 6th ed. Philadelphia, Pa.: Saunders, 1976.

ACTIVITIES

Report on the activities assigned by:

1. Writing a 3–5 page reaction paper (plus assigned charts and diagrams).
2. Using another medium (tape, photography, drawing, etc.) with the consent of the instructor.

1. Observe an early childhood program and comment on the extent to which it seems to you to meet the child's needs for psychological *and* physical safety?

2. Draw a diagram of the indoor and outdoor space in an early childhood program. Comment on how well areas are delineated, how well traffic can flow, ease of observational supervision, and the variety and suitability of equipment and materials. How effective does the arrangement of space seem to be in meeting the needs of the children?

3. Observe the activity areas in a program, using the accompanying "Area Checklist." Are the areas attractive and adequately equipped? Do they facilitate the development of creativity and autonomy?

4. Observe the use of equipment and materials in an early childhood program using the accompanying "Equipment and Materials Checklist." Does it seem to you that there is adequate equipment and materials to facilitate all areas of children's development?

5. Observe the way that time is scheduled in an early childhood program. How effective are the routines and schedule in meeting the needs of the children? What advantages and disadvantages do you see in the way the routines and schedule work? What changes might you make to improve the program's functioning?

6. Plan a daily schedule for an early childhood program in which you think you would enjoy working. Explain your choices in terms of your objectives for children.

Area Checklist

Area	What kind of learning does it facilitate?	Is there a variety of materials?		Are materials attractively displayed?		Does the design facilitate creativity?	Does the design facilitate self-directed use (autonomy)?	Does the design facilitate observation and supervision?
		Yes	*No*	*Yes*	*No*	*How to Improve*	*How to Improve*	*How to Improve*

Equipment and Materials Checklist

What?	Where?		When?			How?	Function
Materials and equipment	Indoors	Outdoors	All times	By daily schedule	Special Activity	How is it used? How many uses?	Social/Emotional Intellectual/Physical

7. Draw a diagram of the way space is arranged in an early child-hood program you are familiar with. On another diagram redesign the use of space in order to make it more effective for learning and/or congruent with your goals for children. Describe the changes you have made and why.

8. Draw a plan for an early childhood classroom in which you think you would enjoy working. Explain your decisions about where areas are located and what equipment is chosen based on your objectives for children.

9. Draw a plan for an outdoor play environment and describe how it would facilitate child growth and development. Indicate the relationship between indoor and outdoor space.

10. If these activities do not challenge you, design your own activity with the consent of the instructor.

DISCUSSION GUIDE

1. Think back to your earliest school experience and think about:
Use of space—how was the space arranged? How did it affect relationships and learning?
Use of equipment and materials—what was in the classroom? How were materials stored and distributed? What were the effects of the use of equipment and materials?
Use of time—was it child-chosen or teacher-chosen? What do you remember of your feelings about the schedule?

2. Choose a setting for young children that you are familiar with and think about:
Provisions made for health and safety—do the routines meet the children's needs for a balance of activity, nourishment, and rest? How do you feel about the way routines are handled?
Use of time—how is time divided between activities? Is it primarily child-chosen or teacher-chosen? What do you feel are the effects of the use of time on relationships and learning?
Use of space—how is space arranged? In what ways does it affect relationships and learning? Does the space arrangement contribute to the accomplishment of the program goals?
Use of equipment and materials—what is in the classroom? How are materials stored and distributed? Do they contribute to the development of autonomy and creativity in children?

RESOURCES

Gross, Dorothy Weisman. "Equipping a Classroom for Young Children," in Katherine Baker Read (Ed.), *Ideas that Work with Young Children*. Washington, D.C.: NAEYC, 1972.

Harms, Thelma. "Evaluating Settings for Learning," in Katherine Baker Read (Ed.), *Ideas That Work with Young Children*. Washington, D.C.: NAEYC, 1972.

Headstart Regional Training Office. "Space for Learning." Washington, D.C.: Department of Health, Education, and Welfare, 1972.

Howes, Virgil M. *Informal Teaching in the Open Classroom*. New York: Macmillan, 1974.

Kritchevsky, Sybil, & Elizabeth Prescott, with Lee Walling. *Physical Space: Planning Environments for Young Children*. Washington, D.C.: NAEYC, 1969.

Prescott, Elizabeth. "Approaches to Quality in Early Childhood Programs." *Childhood Education*, 1974, *50*, 125–131.

Read, Katherine B. *The Nursery School: Human Relationships and Learning*, 6th ed. Philadelphia, Pa.: Saunders, 1976.

Silberman, Charles E. *The Open Classroom Reader*. New York: Random House, 1973.

Stone, Jeannette Galambos. *Play and Playgrounds*. Washington, D.C.: NAEYC, 1970.

Media

Bank Street College of Education. "A Teacher Talks about Her Classroom." Filmstrip. New York: Bank Street College.

Feeney, Stephanie, & Marion Magarick. "Good Toys for Young Children." Slide Filmstrip and Guide. Honolulu, Hawaii: Curriculum Research and Development Group. University of Hawaii, 1976.

SELF-ASSESSMENT

After you have completed the reading, activities, and small-group discussions, look again at the chapter objectives. Write a short paper responding to the following questions.

1. How would you describe your awareness, knowledge, and skill regarding the subject matter of this chapter before you began reading it and doing the activities?

2. To what extent do you feel that you have achieved each of the objectives presented at the beginning of the chapter?

3. What do you see as your strengths in this area?

4. In what specific areas do you need more information and experience? What kinds?

8

Designing Learning Experiences

PURPOSE AND OBJECTIVES

This chapter is intended to help you learn about designing meaningful learning experiences for young children. In it we discuss the relationship between the content and process of learning, introduce curriculum areas usually included in early childhood programs, and discuss how these contribute to the development of the child. We then present an approach to planning activities, describe how curriculum areas can be integrated through the use of themes, and discuss how teachers can communicate with children in ways that support learning. Specifically, the objectives for this chapter are that you:

1. Become aware of the relationship between content and process in learning.
2. Understand the relationship between developmental goals and curriculum areas.
3. Know how early childhood curriculum areas contribute to children's development and some basic approaches to teaching in each area.

4. Understand the value of careful planning of learning experiences based on developmental goals for children.
5. Understand how learning experiences can be related and integrated.
6. Understand how adult communication can support children's learning.

DESIGNING LEARNING EXPERIENCES

The curriculum of the early childhood program consists of a set of learning experiences designed to accomplish developmental goals for children. Curriculum generally has the following characteristics: it is based on a set of values; it takes into account assumptions about how children develop and learn; it has goals (long-term aims), and objectives (specific desired outcomes); it has content; it has a process (method) for communicating the content; and it has means for assessing the extent to which goals and objectives have been met.

In this chapter we use *experiences* as the umbrella term to describe all of the forms of learning that occur in an educational setting—including children's spontaneous play, encounters with people and materials, teacher-designed activities, and all other occasions for learning. The term *activities* is used to refer to teacher-planned opportunities for learning. These may include teacher-directed lessons, games and interest centers designed to achieve specific objectives, and group activities like singing, discussion, and stories.

Relationship between Content and Process in Learning

Young children are learning all the time and from all of their experiences—both in school and out of school. The basic question that the teacher needs to ask herself about facilitating children's learning is, "How, when, and in what ways do I want to intervene in this natural process?"

The role of the teacher of young children is far greater than that of conveying information (in fact, it is a mistake to think that a child necessarily learns something just because we tell it to him.) In a developmental early childhood program, teaching can be seen as building on children's existing interests and motivation, providing experiences, and guiding interactions so as to nurture children's natural curiosity, helping them develop greater understanding of their world, and building positive attitudes toward learning.

In Chapter 2, "Values," we distinguish between process-centered and content-centered programs. Content and process should be viewed as interdependent, for learning cannot take place without something to learn (content) nor without some mode for interaction (process). What varies is the extent to which a teacher emphasizes one or the other and the particular content and process that she chooses.

The ways in which content is communicated in an early childhood program varies with teacher values and goals which determine the extent to which learning is child-initiated or teacher-initiated.

When the emphasis is on child-initiation of learning, teachers take care to design an environment in which children may explore and interact freely. The child's engagement with equipment results in achievement of general developmental goals rather than predetermined objectives.

The process through which children learn in a planned environment is play. Play is an activity performed for its own sake, highly motivated, often involving fantasy, and characterized by intense involvement and concentration. Through play children explore and learn about their world. Play is a rich and varied activity through which many kinds of learning can occur simultaneously. For example, a child playing with blocks may be learning concepts of size, weight and balance, practicing using large and small muscles, expressing his ideas, and cooperating with his peers.

Through play children accomplish some of the most important tasks of their early years. They learn to communicate, to follow rules, to use the tools of their culture, to develop their minds and bodies, and to express and deal with their feelings. Play is sometimes called the child's work because it is such a significant mode of learning. We combine the words play and work into the term *plerk* which we use to describe the intensely involving play learning of young children.

The role of the teacher in play learning is to support the process by providing the environment and materials, and by guiding children's interactions through observing and asking questions which extend their understanding one step further.

Emphasis on teacher-initiation of activities insures the accomplishment of specific learning objectives. In this approach to learning the content consists of curriculum areas usually found in early childhood programs. Areas we will discuss include: sensorimotor experiences, physical development, creative movement, music, art, literature and drama, language, prereading and reading, social studies, math, science, and nutrition and cooking.

The teacher's role in designing activities in these areas may be to present material for children to manipulate, explore and experiment with; to give information; to pose problems and to ask questions that stimulate thought.

The relationship between the content of the early childhood program and the process of achieving developmental goals for children can be graphically portrayed like this:

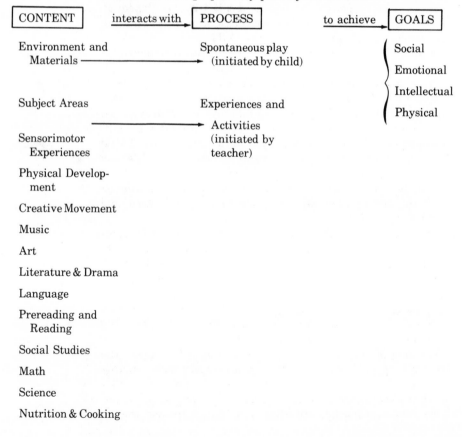

| CONTENT | interacts with | PROCESS | to achieve | GOALS |

Environment and Materials ⟶ Spontaneous play (initiated by child)

Subject Areas

Sensorimotor Experiences

⟶ Experiences and Activities (initiated by teacher)

Social

Emotional

Intellectual

Physical

Physical Development

Creative Movement

Music

Art

Literature & Drama

Language

Prereading and Reading

Social Studies

Math

Science

Nutrition & Cooking

Both approaches to learning are valuable. Most early childhood programs employ both, but the extent to which they are emphasized varies. We know programs in which the great majority of the day is spent allowing children to interact freely with each other and with materials and others that allow children to play spontaneously only when a number of prescribed activities have been completed. The extent to which you rely on the use of a planned environment or predesigned activities is an important choice you will make in planning a program for young children.

In the preceding chapter we explored how the teacher can design an environment to stimulate learning through children's play. In this chapter we will look at how teachers can design curriculum experiences and activities which facilitate children's learning and development.

Curriculum Areas in the Early Childhood Program

Each area of curriculum in the early childhood program can contribute to all areas of the child's development but can be seen as primarily emphasizing one or two areas as shown in the following diagram.

Keep in mind that curriculum areas need not be seen as distinct entities but as natural parts of the life of the child. Remember, too, that all aspects of growth and development are interdependent and that each curriculum area provides opportunities for a number of different kinds of development. For example, a child making a collage is not just engaged in a creative activity, he is also communicating with the teacher and other children, developing skill in solving problems, developing coordination between hand and eye, and exercising the muscles in his fingers and hands.

In this section we present an overview of early childhood curriculum areas. We describe some of the areas usually found in early childhood programs including the teacher's role, the potential for child development and basic concepts. In order to increase your understanding and skill in each of these areas we urge you to read books recommended in the Resource section of this chapter and take workshops and courses which give more specific techniques and practice in presenting curriculum to children.

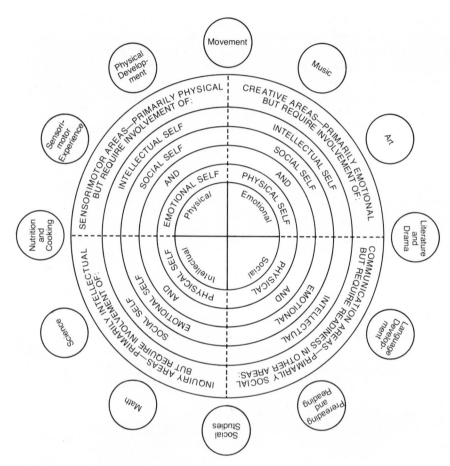

Curriculum Areas That Emphasize
Sensorimotor Development

In the sensorimotor area children need to develop understanding and skill in using their bodies. We put this area first because the child's body is his connector to the world and the senses are the child's primary mode for gathering information. A healthy, strong, flexible, and sensitive body allows a child to function comfortably and competently. Opportunities for using his body and developing his senses give the child awareness of his experience and contribute to his physical development.

Sensorimotor Experiences. Sensorimotor experiences are the core of the curriculum, especially for very young children. These experiences consist of the opportunities that the teacher provides for the child to use all of his senses—to taste, smell, hear, see, touch, and to develop awareness of his body in space.

A field trip to explore the neighborhood gives the child many chances to perceive the world through his senses. As small groups of children walk outside their school the teacher can help them to experience their surroundings and heighten their sensory awareness. They can observe different places and people in the neighborhood; they can smell new smells—a flower, a bakery, or a roof being tarred; and they experience textures as they walk through grass, on asphalt across a gravel road, and feel things along the way—a leaf, an animal, or moss on a rock. Unfamiliar sounds may heighten awareness of hearing—a truck rushing by or the wind blowing through tree tops. As a child climbs a hill and rolls down the other side, or scrambles over a log he experiences distance, depth, and learns about his body in space.

In classrooms teachers can provide sensorimotor experience with activities that require matching, sorting or arranging materials like sound cans, sorting boxes, texture boards, color chips and blocks. Many of the materials found in early childhood programs such as water, sand, mud and paint are excellent sources of sensory exploration. Collections of objects like rocks, shells, leaves, beans, leaves, and buttons give children an opportunity to touch and sort.

Tasting and eating activities provide rich and varied sensory experiences as well as nutrition information for young children who learn from the taste, touch, and smell of food.

Teachers can help children focus on their bodies and their senses by providing materials and experiences, and by talking with children in ways that call attention to what they are doing and experiencing.

Physical Development. A child's ability to use his body and the child's sense of confidence in himself are enhanced as the muscle system becomes strong, flexible, and controlled. A teacher can provide many opportunities for the development of the child's body through equipment, materials, and planned activities.

Physical skill develops when a child has time and space for vigorous activity that involves movement of his arms, legs, and torso. Outdoor play is important in this development. On a well-equipped play yard, children will have space and equipment for swinging, running, throwing, digging, hammering, balancing, and exploring space with their bodies. Indoors, activities like creative movement, rhythmic exercises, balance beams, trampolines, and large blocks can give children the chance to use and develop their bodies. Children develop the small muscles in their hands and fingers through the manipulation of small objects; practicing skills like buttoning, zipping, pouring, writing, painting, and drawing.

Teachers support the development of motor skills when they design an environment and provide children time and direction for physical activities. It is important to observe the abilities and attitudes of the individual child so you can encourage his activity without pushing him toward activities which are beyond his capacity.

Curriculum Areas That Emphasize
Creativity

For teachers who are interested in the development of children who can feel as well as think, and who are sensitive and creative, the arts provide a particularly vital means of expression and communication. Through the arts—creative movement, music, and art, the teacher helps children recognize and express their feelings and responses. Through creative experiences children can express their feelings, communicate their experiences in new forms, and develop their senses and aesthetic appreciation. The child's self-concept is enhanced when his creative expressions are recognized as unique and valuable.

Movement. Creative movement gives children the opportunity to discover the joy and satisfaction of moving in rhythmic and expressive ways. In creative movement activities children are encouraged to find their own personal ways of moving, in contrast to learning a specific dance technique, such as ballet or tap dance. Children learn important social skills as they learn to move in a group without colliding with others and to appreciate and respect each child's individual creative work.

The major role of the teacher in creative movement is to provide a safe, encouraging, and stimulating atmosphere within which children may freely experiment. It is important to establish basic rules for safety (no pushing or bumping; dangerous areas out of bounds) and to model an attitude of respect for individual interpretation and levels of skill.

The basic elements of movement are space, time, and force. Space refers to the physical area in which we move. It includes direction (frontwards, backwards, sideways) and level (high, middle, low). Time refers to the tempo of movement—fast or slow. Force is the amount of energy involved in moving—we can move with great force or very lightly and gently. Children enjoy experiencing time and force in activities involving oppositions—moving very slowly and then very quickly.

Creative movement activities can be quite structured (as children move different parts of their bodies to drumbeat or musical accompaniment) or more open (as children explore all the ways they can work with a prop, such as an old sheet).

Creative movement work is a somewhat difficult area for beginning teachers. The very nature of the activity seems to invite children to become overexcited and out of bounds. Every group of children is different; you will need to experiment with each new group to find out the level of structure that works best for them. Some groups need very specific limits and planned activities; others want lots of time and opportunity to explore broader qualities of movement. Know that in the beginning you will have some very successful sessions and others in which you impose too little or too much structure. The self-awareness that comes out of these experiences can be some of your most valuable learning as a teacher.

Following are some ideas to help you work successfully in your first ventures:

1. Right away, establish a signal such as a drumbeat, "magic" word, hand gesture, on which the children immediately become still. Practice this as a game. By using this signal you can' reduce an activity which is getting too boisterous or dangerous.

2. Keep length of session and group size small. Do not feel that you have to do a forty-minute session in the beginning. Fifteen minutes is fine. If you have more than twelve children in your group, have them alternate moving and watching.

3. Alternate vigorous and quieter activities. Have the children practice an activity sitting down before you let them move freely around the room.

4. End sessions in a way that provides a transition to the next activity. If children are going someplace where they need to be relatively quiet and controlled, help them wind down before they leave the session.

5. If a session goes badly, do not blame the children or yourself. Find a sympathetic friend or colleague with whom you can share and analyze failures or successes.

Do not worry if you are not a trained dancer—you do not need to be in order to enjoy creative movement and to provide valuable movement experiences for children. The basic premise of creative movement work is everyone can enjoy dancing. However, if you have the opportunity to work in dance or movement yourself, under the guidance of an accepting and encouraging teacher, by all means do so. You will find the experience immeasurably helpful in your own teaching.

Music. Because of its enormously expressive quality, music offers a direct route to children's feelings and provides many possibilities for creative expression. Musical experiences for children can include singing, listening, playing instruments, and making up songs and rhythms of their own. Through these experiences children develop the ability to listen and respond to music as an art form. They also begin to develop awareness and understanding of the elements of music including beat, pitch, and melody. Group music experiences can allow the teacher to introduce a new song, guide children in exploring musical elements, and give them experience listening and participating. Group sessions work best with between twelve and fifteen children sitting in a circle. The teacher can accompany songs and activities with simple chords on a guitar or autoharp or the rhythms of a drum or hand clapping. Piano accompaniment removes the teacher from the group and can make it difficult to maintain an intimate atmosphere. A teacher can encourage children's spontaneous musical activities by providing records for them to listen to and musical instruments for them to experiment with every day.

As with movement, music can be a difficult curriculum area for a teacher who doesn't feel comfortable singing and playing. It is not necessary to be a talented musician in order to provide musical experiences in your classroom. It is helpful to remember that children are not harsh judges and can simply enjoy musical activities that they do with the teacher and other children. If you do have skill in singing or playing you may enrich the children's musical experience by singing with them often and teaching them songs that you enjoy.

Art. Art is an important part of the early childhood program because it offers a medium for children to express their understanding and feelings about themselves and their world. Children begin to develop aesthetic awareness and appreciation when they are introduced to good art—either in its original form or in reproductions. The teacher's role is to provide ex-

periences, materials, and relationships which support children's artistic expression and aesthetic appreciation.

The first raw material for artistic expression is experience.

> Children cannot create out of a vacuum. They must have something to say and be fired to say it. More time spent in experiencing richly what they are going to express will bear fruit in deeper involvement in the artistic expression. (Cole, 1940, p. 3)

Direct experiences heighten the child's awareness of his senses and enrich his knowledge about the world. A visit to the beach, to the bakery, to observe a new litter of kittens, or a beautiful display of shells all give inspiration for artistic expression.

In an art program for young children the teacher provides materials for three basic types of activities.

1. Painting and drawing with a variety of media—tempera, finger paints, water colors, crayons, chalk, and felt pens.
2. Printing and collage activities which involve applying one medium to another.
3. Activities using clay, wood, wire, and boxes, to make three-dimensional constructions.

Children need lots of time to explore and experiment with materials. They may work with a particular material for a long time before they discover all its possibilities and have something to express that can be done best in that medium. The best art materials for children—like paint and clay—lend themselves to many types of creative use. All art materials chosen for young children should allow the child to make as many choices as possible about how to use the material.

If an activity is teacher-created and requires the child to follow a predetermined pattern it should be considered a craft and not art. Teacher-created activities which result in uniform products (all-alike Santa's with stuck-on cotton beards) may be useful for developing small motor skills and the ability to follow directions, but they do not foster creative expression.

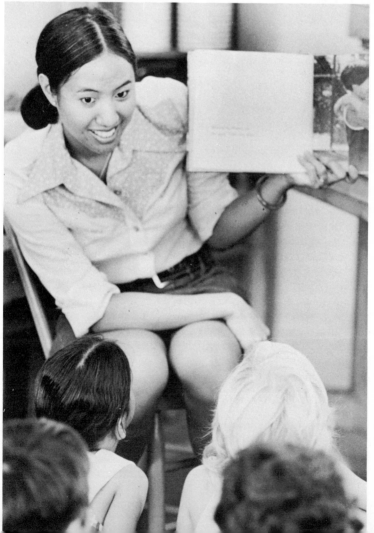

Literature and Drama. Literature uses language to portray feelings, ideas, and experiences. Literature for children consists of stories, poems, plays and tales, legends and myths.

Through literature children can experience events from the past, the present, and ideas about the future. Other lives, cultures, and places become available to them. They are exposed to fantasy worlds which are peopled by frightening, delightful, and magical creatures and in which unfamiliar or impossible events occur. The artful use of words and creative imagination helps children enjoy the rhythm and flow of their language and stimulates their desire to create literature of their own.

To help children understand and enjoy literature the teacher provides opportunities for them to experience stories, poems and plays. As a teacher, you can do this by selecting, displaying and using books that fit the interests and developmental levels of the children.

The following suggestions are intended to help you make a good selection of stories and poems for a classroom.

1. Include both new and traditional favorites.

2. Select a mixture of stories, poetry, rhymes, and folk tales that deal with both the familiar and fantasy worlds.

3. Include books that reflect the interests of the children in your classroom.

4. Include the literature of different ethnic groups, cultures, and regions of the world, and be sure to reflect the ethnic and cultural backgrounds of the children in the group.

5. Choose books which show men, women, girls, and boys in a variety of roles.

6. Select books for the lively, interesting illustrations that support a story which develops an idea through action and character. (Avoid books of fancy illustrations that hide a boring or moralizing story.)

7. Include books that have received awards and prizes such as the Newbery Medal and the National Book Award if they are suitable to the developmental level and interests of the children.

The books you select should be thoughtfully arranged so that reading is an inviting and pleasurable experience. A library area that is well-lit, full of pillows, rugs, plants, art, and a well-displayed, varied, and constantly changing supply of books will be inviting for children. It will be a place where groups of children can relax and enjoy hearing good literature read by their teacher or other willing adults.

The literature experiences provided through good books, can be expanded into storytelling and puppetry, and dramatic presentations. Children can be encouraged to act out their favorites, create their own stories, dictate them to the teacher, and illustrate them with their own art work. Children may enjoy making their own puppets and puppet stage and presenting a play based on a favorite story or their own experiences.

Curriculum Areas That Emphasize Communication

Through their ability to communicate, children convey their thoughts and needs, interact with others, and learn about the world they live in.

Communication skills, (often called *language arts* in the elementary school curriculum) have four components: listening, speaking, reading, and writing. Listening and reading are receptive in nature and allow children to gather information about the world, while speaking and writing allow them to express their feelings and ideas. Curriculum areas in the early childhood program that contribute to communication skills are language and prereading and reading.

Language. The child brings his language with him to school and it is the role of the teacher to extend and enrich it. The teacher helps a child learn language by showing respect for the language he speaks and the way he speaks it; by making lots of time for language to happen in the classroom; by listening to the child and encouraging him to talk about his ideas, feelings and activities; by providing experiences which children can discuss; and by providing a model of fluent and interesting speech.

Language cannot be isolated from other areas of the curriculum. Nearly every activity that a child does in school involves language. The teacher can aid in language development by providing a classroom that is full of materials and experiences that are interesting and which provide many and varied opportunities for children to use language.

Children practice language as they interact with objects and people in the classroom and through the social interactions in the block corner, sandbox, water table, art area, and at snacks and meals. One of the richest centers for language is the dramatic play area where children practice the roles and speech of the important people in their lives. Another important way to stimulate language is through reading and discussing books. Language development can be enhanced by commercial language curricula like the Peabody Language Kits and Distar Language Program, which may be useful supplements but not a substitute for a language rich classroom.

Every part of the day can be full of language experiences if children are allowed to talk about their activities and interests. The thing most likely to interfere with children's language development is a teacher who does all the talking herself or restricts children's social interactions and dialogue.

Prereading and Reading. Reading is one facet of communication—a tool to unlock ideas, adventures, and relationships and not a skill to be mastered for its own sake.

For the last twenty years a lively debate has gone on over when children should be taught to read. From the developmental perspective it is not possible to generalize about when all children should learn. Early childhood programs can build interest and motivation and provide opportunities for children to develop the prerequisite skills for reading.

Before a child learns to read he needs experience in the world to give him a basis for understanding what he reads and the ability to comprehend and use language.

A teacher who wishes to encourage reading will have available in her classroom a variety of materials and activities designed to develop the skills (sometimes called *reading readiness*) which are important prerequisites for reading. These skills include large and small motor development, visual discrimination, auditory discrimination, problem-solving, sequencing, and left-to-right orientation.

Important ways to stimulate children's interest in reading

are to read many children's books, and to demonstrate your own appreciation of books and your enjoyment in reading.

The teacher prepares the actual path for reading by helping children to realize what words stand for things. For example, if the teacher and children label objects in the classroom and discuss the labels, then children begin to understand this concept. Another way that the teacher can help children see that reading is talk written down and assist in beginning reading is by having them dictate stories and captions for their paintings.

We have seen early childhood teachers successfully use Sylvia Ashton-Warner's technique of having children dictate words that have meaning for their lives. The teacher writes these words on cards which become the "key vocabulary" for many reading activities such as games and stories. Ashton-Warner's book *Teacher* can provide the information and inspiration for using this technique.

Curriculum Areas That Emphasize the Development of Inquiry

Young children are constantly developing concepts about the physical world and how it works, about the social world they live in, and about the inner world of feelings. The way the child organizes his experiences in the world to make them useful to him is through the development of *concepts*. A concept can be defined as a mental structure which represents a group of things or ideas that have common characteristics.

Inquiry is the process of organizing experience through exploring, building, and testing ideas about the world. It is through these processes of inquiry that the young child generates his concepts of the physical and social world. These inquiry processes include:

> *Exploring*—using the senses to observe, investigate, and manipulate;
>
> *Identifying*—naming and describing what one experiences;
>
> *Classifying*—grouping the common properties of objects or experiences;
>
> *Comparing & Contrasting*—observing similarities and differences between objects or experiences;

Hypothesizing—using the data from experiences to make guesses (hypotheses) about what might happen;

Generalizing—applying previous experience to new events.

Concepts can deal with the physical world of the child (called math or science in the curriculum) or with the social and emotional world of the child (referred to as social studies).

Social Studies. Social studies offers the child the opportunity to explore the relationships between people, and between people and their environment. The teacher can use the most basic question in the child's life—Who Am I?—as an organizing framework for social studies activities. Through this question the child can see the relevance of activities to his own life, gain self-awareness and acquire beginning concepts from the social and behavioral sciences. In the following paragraphs six organizing questions and the social science fields they relate to are presented followed by some basic teaching strategies for introducing social studies to young children.

Who Am I as a Person with Feelings? In this area teachers of young children help them accept and deal with their feelings and learn to handle them in constructive ways. Also, teachers help children with the important task of the preschool years— learning to distinguish fantasy from reality. The social science field that relates to this area is psychology.

Who Am I as a Member of a Family? In this area the child learns about himself as a member of a family, and how families meet the needs of people, both in his community and in other communities around the world. Anthropology and sociology are social science fields that relate to this area.

Who Am I as a Member of a Community? In this area children learn about their community: the people in it, what they do, how people get the goods and services they need, and how rules are made to protect the members of the community. The social science fields that relate to this area are economics, political science, and sociology.

Who Am I as a Part of a Race and Culture? Teachers can help children realize that they are people first, with things in common with all people and that their cultural background is something that enhances who they are. Children can become aware of and develop pride in their own race and cultural heritage while learning that differences between races and cultures contribute to a society which is rich and interesting. The social science field of anthropology deals with this area.

Who Am I as a Person in a Place? In an early childhood program teachers can help children gain awareness of how they are linked with other living things and with the natural features of their environment. Geography and ecology are the related fields.

Who Am I as a Person in Time? In the early childhood program young children can begin to develop awareness of time sequence and learn about events that happened in the past. The field of history deals with this area.

As a teacher you can provide many social studies experiences based on the background and activities of the children in your classroom. To do this you must know about the child, his family, their ethnic and cultural backgrounds, their role in the community, and what interests and concerns they have. You will also have the opportunity to share things you are interested in and care about with children. Because social studies is such a broad area and can be approached in such diverse ways, it is an excellent umbrella under which to organize and integrate all other subject areas. Strategies effective in introducing social studies to young children include experiences in the classroom such as songs, dances, food preparation, visitors, and books. Direct experiences in the world, such as community field trips, are an excellent way to provide social studies experiences. In the classroom there can be follow-up activities in every area of curriculum including role-playing, art work, dictating stories, songs, and constructing things that represent the experiences. The design of activities and the kinds of questions the teacher asks will stimulate the children to inquire about and integrate their experiences.

Mathematics. In the early childhood program mathematics is much more than counting and recognizing shapes. Math is a way for the young child to organize and understand the physical world. Some areas of mathematical learning for young children are the development of concepts of classification, space, number, measurement, ordering, and time.

Experience with *classification* happens all the time in a classroom as children group things together based on the common characteristics of color, shape, size, use, and other qualities. Children are learning to group things according to their common attributes when they put all the sand toys in one bucket and all the water toys in another, when they hang the dresses up and place the hats in a drawer, and when they place all the large beads in a basket and all the small beads in a can.

Children develop concepts about *space* like location, direction, and distance as they move in space and notice the relationship of their bodies to the physical world.

Learning about *numbers* involves a great deal more than being able to count. Counting may be only a memorization activity unless the child has a concept of number (oneness, twoness, threeness) attached to the words so that he knows what the symbol represents in the physical world. Number concepts include comparison (more, less, same), position (first, second, third), one-to-one correspondence (one cup for each saucer, a napkin for each person), and sets (two or more objects that belong together).

Measurement is the process of comparing a quantity against some standard. Examples are how many cups of water fill the larger container in the water table or how many unit blocks equal the width of the room.

Ordering (seriation) takes place when objects are arranged in a sequence based on a difference such as size, texture, or shading. Children gain experience in ordering when they arrange themselves from shortest to tallest or when they arrange a set of color chips from palest pink to darkest pink.

Time concepts can be developed as children notice the sequence of events in their daily lives; for example, rest time always follows lunch time or "Today we will read a story about the zoo, tomorrow we will go there to see the animals."

To help children learn mathematical concepts the teacher needs to provide materials for the child to explore such as blocks, sand, water, math blocks, rulers, beads, and many other objects which help them focus on math concepts and to ask questions using mathematical language.

Science. Children are constantly observing the world, exploring it, and asking questions about why and how things happen. Science is a process of observing, identifying the properties of things, discovering the relationships between things and searching for the answers to the "why" questions. Science for young children is an active process.

Science experiences for young children can be divided into three broad categories: biological science, earth and space science, and physical science.

Biological science is the study of living things—what they are, how they live, and their life cycles.

Earth and space science is the study of our planet—the passing of day and night, the seasons, the presence of sun, moon, earth, stars, air and water, and the study of weather.

Physical science is the study of matter and change. It includes daily things that children experience like light, sound, temperature, magnetism, and electricity.

As a teacher your role in helping children learn about science is to encourage the observing, questioning, and problem-solving processes by providing experiences with the raw materials of science study, by providing resources and information to learn more about these things, and to model questioning behaviors and strategies for finding answers to questions.

Nutrition and Cooking. Nutrition and cooking activities integrate learning in many curriculum areas, lend themselves to active involvement, and are very interesting to children because they are so closely related to the everyday experiences of eating and watching food preparation. To actually get to clean, chop, measure, combine, and cook foods is a very exciting activity for children.

Children can become aware of and begin to understand how the foods they eat contribute to their growth, energy level, and health. They can learn that all foods contain nutrients in the form of vitamins, minerals, proteins, fats, and carbohydrates, that some foods contain more of these than others, and that their bodies need a certain amount of nutrients daily to stay healthy. Children are often delighted to learn that the bread they eat for lunch contains carbohydrates that gives them energy to run and play and the peanut butter on their sandwich provides some of the proteins their body cells need in order to grow.

Nutrition and cooking activities can provide the opportunity for integrating a number of different curriculum areas. Children develop *mathematical* concepts and skills when they measure, weigh, divide, sort and classify foods while cooking. *Science* learning occurs as children combine ingredients, observe how they change as they are cooked, and see the effects of things like leavening, and temperature on foods. Nurturing a school garden can stimulate inquiry about science and nutrition. A child can observe and learn that the vegetables and fruits in the school garden need the nutrients from the soil, water, and sun for growth and health as much as his body needs minerals, vitamins, proteins, fats, and carbohydrates provided in foods. *Language* develops as children talk about their cooking experiences and hear the words for different foods, utensils, equipment and cooking processes. Children gain *social studies* concepts as they explore how foods get to them and as they cook and eat foods from different cultures. As children taste, smell, feel, and see foods, they have many *sensory experiences*. Children can read books and sing about food as well as use food as a theme for art projects.

A classroom center for cooking activities can be set-up for individual or small groups (4–6) of children. Cooking activities with children should be planned to include: equipment and materials needed, how to locate and set-up, and how to conduct the activity for maximum involvement and safety. Books in the resource section of this chapter provide guidelines for set-up and use of a cooking center.

Planning Activities for Children

This section presents an approach to planning activities for children that support their development as moving, thinking, communicating, and creating people. Planning will help you to be clear about the purposes of the experiences you offer children and how these relate to your developmental goals. When you have your goals clearly in mind, you define the specific awareness, understanding, or skill that you wish children to acquire, such as understanding concepts of number or location, hand-eye coordination, recognition of primary colors, or awareness of the kinds of life found by the sea. Next you plan experiences intended to accomplish your objectives. The final step in the planning process is to assess the effectiveness of the activity in terms of the goals and objectives.

In order to check if the activities you plan for children are purposeful, it is useful to ask yourself the following question, "If someone were to walk into my classroom right now and ask me why I am doing this activity, would I be able to give a good reason for it?" We have asked this question of teachers and often found that they were unable to explain their reason for presenting an activity except that it seemed like a good idea or that the children seemed to enjoy it. It is possible to plan experiences for children which they enjoy *and* which contribute to their development.

The figure which follows represents three steps in the planning process. You may start in any of these places and progress around the circle. Where you begin will depend on the type of program you teach in and your particular purpose.

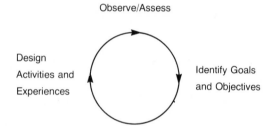

Observe/Assess

Design Activities and Experiences

Identify Goals and Objectives

Planning may begin with observation and assessment of an individual child or group of children. This may be accomplished through the use of informal observation of children's skills and understandings or by using a predesigned assessment instrument like the checklists found in *School Before Six: A Diagnostic Approach* (Hodgden, 1974), or the *Portage Kit* (Blume et al., 1976). After observing and assessing children's areas of strength and weakness the teacher formulates learning objectives and designs experiences and activities to achieve these objectives.

Planning may also begin with a set of objectives selected from a packaged early childhood curriculum like the *Peabody Language Development Kit* (Dunn and Smith, 1965), the *DISTAR* Language Program (Engelmann and Osborne, 1969) or from objectives developed by the staff or administration of your school. If your planning begins with predetermined objectives, you then present the activities which accompany the objectives

in the published curriculum or design your own activities to accomplish the objectives. You then observe and assess to see if the objectives have been achieved and when it is time to move on to the next set of objectives and activities.

Finally, planning may begin with the design of an activity based on the interests or concerns of the children, for example, animals, a new television show, the birth of a baby, or a shared experience like a trip or play. You can observe this type of activity to see how the children respond and then decide how to extend the activity to further the learning.

The various starting places in the planning process can be adapted for programs which emphasize content or process. In a more process-centered program the teacher is most likely to begin with the interests and concerns of the children, and in a more content-centered program learning objectives are most likely to be specified in advance to focus on acquisition of knowledge or skill.

Writing Plans for Activities

Written plans are very helpful for organizing and guiding activities for children. A teacher with many years of experience may be able to plan successful activities in her head without writing them down, but mastering the planning process first is essential. A good activity planning outline helps. Such a plan includes all of the steps necessary to be fully prepared, is convenient to use (we print an activity planning form on 5″ × 8″ cards for easy storage and retrieval), and is not so detailed that you get bogged down when you try to follow it. When you first begin to present activities to children it is a good idea to practice first and memorize the steps as much as possible so you can give full attention to your interaction with the children. A written plan provides you with a useful guideline to follow but you need not be rigidly tied to it. If you get an inspiration from the children in midstream, redirecting the activity often works as well as the original plan.

Written objectives are an important part of the planning process because they help you to focus on the specific outcomes that you are trying to achieve and help you assess whether you have been successful in reaching these intended outcomes. Objectives should be written as specifically as possible and stated in terms of the behavior that you want children to be able to demonstrate. Objectives for children can be described in each developmental area: social, emotional, intellectual, and physical.

Though it is useful to gain focus through the use of objectives, it is also important not to get so committed to the achievement of the objectives that it gets between you and a meaningful interaction with a child. If the child is not ready or has other more pressing concerns, it may be best to abandon or revise an activity and deal with the child's immediate interest or need.

A sample of the Activity Planning Form that we have designed for our student's use and a brief description of how it can be used is on page 231.

Activity Planning Form

Curriculum Area _____Date _____
Brief Description of Activity: _____

(What are you going to do? How will the activity be set up?)

Assessment/Rationale:

(Why are you choosing to carry on this activity with this group of children at this time?)

GOALS	OBJECTIVES
Social/Emotional	_____
Intellectual	Concepts to be learned
	_____
	Vocabulary
	_____
Physical	Small Muscle
	_____
	Large Muscle
	_____
	Sensory
	_____

Materials Needed:

(Exactly what materials will you need? Don't forget provision for protection of clothes and clean-up.)

Introduction:

(How will you introduce the activity? What will you say or do to get the children's interest and to let them know what they will be doing?)

Procedure:

(Step-by-step description of the activity)

Evaluation/Follow-up:

(What was the children's response? What might be changed so that the activity might have been more successful? Did you notice any potential for follow-up activities based on what the children said or did?)

The following tips for planning activities will often help avert disaster:

- Check each activity planned to make sure that the children understand the words and concepts that you introduce.
- Give children plenty of opportunity to explore the materials you are going to use prior to the activity.
- Write your plans on cards and keep them on file for future use. (You won't regret it!)

Remember that the better thought out the planning is the more comfortable you will be and the better the experience will be for you and for the children.

Themes for Integrating Experiences

Using themes (sometimes called units) to organize and integrate learning experiences gives focus to the teacher's planning and deepens and extends children's ability to gain meaning from their experiences. Sources for these themes can come from the children, the teacher, or existing curricula.

The ethnic and cultural background of the children is a rich source of themes for organizing experiences. For example, a team of Head Start teachers in Hawaii used the varied cultural and ethnic backgrounds of children in their class (Chinese, Japanese, Samoan, Hawaiian, and Filipino) to organize experiences for an entire year. As they focused on each culture in turn they learned words and phrases from the language, saw traditional costumes, read stories, played games, did art and craft activities, and did songs and dances. They also cooked and snacked on ethnic foods and handled household objects from the culture studied. The teachers used the resources of their classroom community by asking the families to bring their knowledge of their heritage into the classroom. The cultural themes contributed to the children's awareness and understanding of the larger world, heightened their sense of uniqueness and pride, and built a sense of community with participating families. While these larger goals were being realized the children were also developing skills and understandings in all of the subjects usually included in early childhood programs.

Another way of organizing curriculum is by studying the community through field trips. This method is used by the laboratory school of Bank Street College of Education in New York City as the major focus of their curriculum for children. Field trips, used as themes for organizing curriculum, are carefully planned and have extensive follow-up activities as contrasted to trips we remember from childhood which had no preparation and no follow-up except a thank you letter. For example, when children take a trip to the tide pools, teachers begin the preparation by discussion of what they will see and do and may share a relevant story or film. On the trip the teacher pays careful attention to the children's interests and their questions. When they return the class may spend several days or weeks on follow-up activities based on the trip and the children's questions. These may include drawing pictures of what they saw and dictating stories about their pictures, classifying and counting what they found, reading books about shore life, dissecting a shellfish, cooking with fish or seaweed, building a model tide pool in plaster of paris, and doing creative drama activities about the seashore.

Another kind of integrating theme is a concept such as size, shape, food, family, or community helpers. A group of teachers in a program we have worked with used food as the integrating theme for a series of activities planned over a two month period. Children and teachers created many math, science, social studies, art, drama, language, cooking, and sensory experiences around the concept of food.

Field trips were planned to a dairy, a commercial fishing boat, a local farmer's market, a chicken farm and the supermarket. On these trips the children learned many things about where the foods they ate came from and how they were processed and distributed. Back in the classroom the children painted and drew pictures about their experiences and wrote stories to accompany the pictures.

Many of the children brought fruits from home such as bananas, papayas, mangos, and limes. These children shared how the fruits grew and were harvested and joined their friends in preparing school snacks of fruit salads and fruit smoothies.

A school vegetable garden provided opportunities for physical and intellectual experiences as the children prepared the ground and planted vegetables. In tending the garden they learned about the importance of soils, light, and water in the growth of plants.

One teacher and a group of children planned, shopped for, and cooked a huge pot of stew. The children had many social and language experiences in their discussions about what they could put in it, how and where they could get the ingredients, and how the foods they used would be good for them. Each child chose an ingredient to shop for. Many math experiences occurred as they decided on quantities, weighed, purchased their ingredients, and counted the change. After preparing the stew and serving it to the whole school for lunch the group did a dramatization of the process—each child acted out his own ingredient as it went into the pot and boiled and blended with all of the other ingredients.

Finally, the daily experiences of the children can be a source of themes. These may emerge from the children's interests or from a shared experience. For example, a hike on a windy hill with a group of children led another creative teacher we know into an in-depth exploration of wind. Her class made wind mills, kites and weather vanes, explored the effects of wind on their surroundings, read stories about wind and eventually became interested in the study of weather.

As you can see the sources for themes and the possibilities for integrating experiences is rich and endlessly varied. When integrating themes are used thoughtfully they can provide children with new knowledge and serve as an organizing focus for many other curriculum areas. A danger in the use of themes is that developmental goals for children can get lost in a flurry of activities designed by the teacher to deal with the theme.

The ways in which teachers interact with children have important implications for relationships, the development of inquiry and creativity, and the amount of autonomy the child experiences as a learner. In this section we will look at four areas in which teacher communication can support children's learning. These include initiation of interactions, types of questions, time allowed for children's responses, and teacher's responses to children.

Communication That Supports Children's Learning

Initiation of Interactions

Do most conversations and activities in the classroom begin with the teacher or do they begin with the children? What is the balance between the two? If teachers initiate all interactions and monopolize the talk in the classroom children may not be able to express their interests and concerns. In settings in which there is a balance between teacher- and child-initiated interactions, children are learning that adults value their interests and wish to encourage their independence.

Types of Questions

The kinds of questions that teachers ask can be either open or closed. A closed question is one that has only one correct or acceptable answer. For example, "What color is this bead?" "Is this box open or closed?" "Is this a circle?" Closed questions are effective for gathering information as to whether children have acquired a concept or a piece of information as well as for gathering information quickly and efficiently.

Open questions stimulate inquiry and they encourage children to explore further. They can be answered in a number of different ways and have more than one correct answer. An open question says to the child, "Tell me more." You can develop skill in asking open questions when you are aware of their value and are willing to practice until you can do it comfortably. Following are examples of open questions which facilitate inquiry:

What do you see? (hear, feel, smell)

How are these the same? (different)

What do you think about ... ?

How do you know ... ?

What do you think would happen if ... ?

How do you think we could find out ... ?

In most classrooms teachers will use a mixture of open and closed questions. The mix will be influenced by values, objectives and the nature of the particular situation. Awareness of the usefulness of each type of question can help you make more conscious choices about what kinds of questions to use to accomplish your goals for children.

Time Allowed for Response

The amount of silence that a teacher allows between statements or questions is an important factor in how children respond. Researchers have found that three to five seconds is the average amount of silence that occurs between teacher questions and learner response or a follow-up comment from the teacher. They found that if the teacher waits only one or two seconds, she gets one-word responses from the children. If she waits for several seconds longer, children will respond with whole sentences, and complete thoughts which represent more creativity and increased speculativeness (Costa, 1974, p. 60). If you wish to stimulate inquiry, you need to be aware of the impact of the time allowed for the child to think and respond to your question.

Responses to Children

Teachers can respond to children's talk and their activities in evaluative or nonevaluative ways. Criticism and praise are forms of evaluation and are consistent with a program that is based on a belief in external motivation of the child. Description and clarification are nonevaluative responses to children's work which are consistent with a view that learning is based largely on internal motivation.

Evaluative Responses. Criticism implies finding fault or judging negatively. Teachers often criticize children for incorrect responses or for work that does not achieve a set standard.

The assumption underlying criticism is that if a child knows he is incorrect or that his work is inadequate, he will correct himself or work harder. Often criticism has a negative effect, and it may result in the child feeling inadequate or responding by withdrawal or defensiveness.

Although praise is usually regarded as a very effective technique for encouraging children, it can have unforeseen negative effects. Using praise to reward children for their efforts and accomplishments often causes them to work for the praise rather than for the satisfaction inherent in what they are doing. Praise which is premature may result in the child's stopping his efforts long before he has realized the potential of an activity. Children also know when the teacher is lavishing praise on something he knows is not his best work and when she indiscriminately praises everything and everyone until it has no meaning. Children can also see an implied criticism in praise for if something can be praised, it can also be criticized. If you tell a child he is "good," you may as easily judge him bad, or if you enthusiastically praise a child's use of bright colors in his painting, he may continue to paint similar pictures to gain your praise. He may not risk the possibility of criticism that could come if he explored further and mixed the paints together until they become muddy.

Nonevaluative Responses. Teachers who value the child's understanding and thought more than the acquisition of correct answers will strive to clarify rather than evaluate children's statements and answers. Clarifying consists of restating what the child has just said in order to check whether you have understood it. When you reflect back your understanding of what the child has said, it gives him a chance to see if his words adequately communicated his ideas and allows him to elaborate if he wishes.

Teachers can respond to children's art work, building, and other activities by describing what they see instead of evaluating. A child may be more likely to continue exploring and experimenting when you describe his actions and the effect on you. For example, "It's interesting how the blue and green are blending together in your picture," or "I see you have left lots of white spaces on your painting," rather than, "What a beautiful picture," or "Why don't you fill in all that white space?"

When a teacher regularly uses nonevaluative communication, she creates an environment in which children feel safe to take risks and go further into the process of learning.

REFERENCES

Ashton-Warner, Sylvia. *Teacher*. New York: Simon & Schuster, 1963.

Blume, Susan, et al. *Portage Guide to Early Education*. Portage, Wisc.: Cooperative Educational Service Agency, 1976.

Carr, Albert. "Science in the Elementary School: A Humanistic Approach." *Educational Perspectives, 10,* Honolulu, Hawaii, 1971.

Cole, Natalie Robinson. *The Arts in the Classroom*. New York: John Day, 1940.

Costa, Arthur. *Basic Teaching Behaviors*. San Anselmo, Calif.: Search Models Unlimited, 1974.

Dunn, Lloyd, and Smith, James. *Peabody Language Development Kits*. Circle Pines, Minn.: American Guidance Service, 1965.

Engelmann, Siegfried; Osborn, Jean; and Engelmann, Therese. *Distar Language*. Chicago, Ill.: Science Research Associate, 1969.

Feeney, Stephanie. "A Learner-Centered Approach to Early Reading Experiences for Young Children," in Malcolm P. Douglas, (Ed.), *Clarement Reading Conference 40th Yearbook*. Claremont, Calif.: Claremont Reading Conference, 1976.

Feeney, Stephanie. *Child Development Associate Module: Social Studies*. Honolulu, Hawaii: Curriculum Research and Development Group, 1975.

Hartley, Ruth E. *Understanding Children's Play*. New York: Columbia University Press, 1952.

Hodgden, Laurel, et al. *School Before Six: A Diagnostic Approach*. St. Louis, Mo.: CEMREL, Inc., 1974.

Magarick, Marion, *Child Development Associate Module: Creative Movement*. Honolulu, Hawaii: Curriculum Research and Development Group, 1975.

Spodek, Bernard (Ed.). *Play: The Child Strives Toward Self-Actualization*. Washington, D. C.: NAEYC, 1971.

Sponseller, Doris (Ed.). *Play as a Learning Medium*. Washington, D. C.: NAEYC, 1974.

Streets, Donald, and Jordon, Daniel. *Guiding the Process of Becoming: The Anisa Theories of Curriculum and Teaching*. Wilmette, Ill.: World Order, 1973.

ACTIVITIES

Report on the activities assigned by:

1. Writing a 3–5 page reaction paper.
2. Using another medium (tape, photography, drawing, etc.) with the instructor's consent.

   1. Observe a child engaged in an activity that was self-selected and that you would define as play. Describe the way the child interacted with the material, the level of involvement, the kinds of feelings the child seemed to be having, the role of the teacher, and what the child might have been learning. What did you learn about children and play?

   2. Write an imaginary dialogue between a preschool teacher and a parent who is upset because what his child does in school is play all day instead of learning something useful.

   3. Observe a teacher-directed learning activity. What do you believe the goals and objectives for the activity might be? How does the activity contribute to the accomplishment of the goals? Do you believe the activity was successful in accomplishing its purpose?

   4. Observe a classroom for experiences that contribute to sensorimotor development. To what extent do the experiences contribute to health and sensorimotor development?

   5. Observe a classroom and note the kinds of communication experiences available to children. To what extent do they seem effective in helping the children become competent in using language to communicate their thoughts and feelings?

   6. Observe a classroom and note the creative experiences available to children. To what extent do the experiences offered seem to contribute to the development of creativity?

7. Observe a classroom and note the kinds of learning experiences that are intended to develop inquiry. To what extent are the experiences successful in facilitating inquiry in the children?

8. Use the "Activity Planning Form" (p. 231) to practice planning an activity for children in any curriculum area you choose. Implement with children if possible and evaluate.

9. Design a unit based on a theme. Specify the theme, describe your goals for children, specific objectives for reaching these goals, and how curriculum areas can be integrated. Implement with children if possible and evaluate.

10. Observe a teacher and describe the kinds of questions she uses, the amount of time she allows for children to respond to questions, and the ways she responds to children (evaluative and nonevaluative). How effective are her communications in facilitating learning? What does her communication suggest about her beliefs regarding motivation for learning and why?

11. Tape 10–15 minutes of classroom interaction in which you play an instructional role. Analyze your interaction in terms of—
who initiates the communications,
the kinds of questions you used, and
the way you responded to the children's talk.
Describe the effects of your communication in stimulating inquiry. Describe how your communication could have been more effective in supporting the child's learning.

12. If these activities do not challenge you, design your own activity with the consent of the instructor.

DISCUSSION GUIDE

1. What was your favorite kind of play as a young child? How might it have contributed to your development?

2. What are your feelings about the role of play in the lives of children, in your own life?

3. Recall your earliest school experiences and share your memories about the following:
The kinds of learning experiences your teachers provided.
Evidence of a planning process.
Use of integrating themes (units).
Kinds of teacher communication used to facilitate learning.

4. How were the learning experiences planned and organized in the early childhood programs you have visited? What do you believe the goals and objectives might have been? Did the experiences seem to accomplish these goals and objectives?

5. Describe the planning process you have observed in a program you have visited.

6. Describe the kinds of themes (units) you have observed and your reactions to them.

7. In early childhood programs you have observed, what kinds of communication took place concerning learning experiences? In what ways did teacher communication seem to support or discourage creativity and inquiry in children?

RESOURCES

Amazing Life Games Company. *The Amazing Life Games Theater.* Boston: Houghton Mifflin, 1971.

Ashton-Warner, Sylvia. *Teacher.* New York: Simon & Schuster, 1963.

Bank Street College of Education. *Community as Classroom* (sound filmstrip). New York: Bank Street College.

Baratta-Lorton, Mary. *Workjobs.* Menlo Park, Calif.: Addison-Wesley, 1972.

Barlin, Anne, and Barlin, Paul. *The Art of Learning Through Movement.* Los Angeles: Ward Ritchie Press, 1971.

Blume Susan, et al. *Portage Guide to Early Education.* Portage, Wisc.: Cooperative Educational Service Agency, 1976.

Braun, Samuel, et al. *Curriculum is What Happens.* Washington, D.C.: NAEYC, 1970.

Carmichael, Viola. *Science Experiences for Young Children.* Los Angeles, Calif.: Southern California Association for the Education of Young Children, 1969.

Cherry, Claire. *Creative Art for the Developing Child.* Belmont, Calif.: Fearon Publishers, 1972.

Cook, Ann. *Cooking in the Open Classroom: An Integrated Activity.* New York: City University of New York, 1971.

Copeland, Richard. *Diagnostic and Learning Activities in Mathematics for Children.* New York: Macmillan, 1974.

Engelmann, Siegfried; Osborn, Jean; and Engelmann, Therese. *Distar Language.* Chicago, Ill.: Science Research Associate, 1969.

Goodwin, Mary, and Pollen, Gerry. *Creative Food Experiences for Children.* Washington, D.C.: Center for Science in the Public Interest, 1974.

Harlan, Jean. *Science Experiences for the Early Childhood Years.* Columbus, Ohio: Charles E. Merrill, 1976.

Hartley, Ruth E. *Understanding Children's Play.* New York: Columbia University Press, 1952.

Hodgden, Laurel, et al. *School Before Six: A Diagnostic Approach.* St. Louis, Mo.: CEMREL, 1974.

Holt, Bess-Gene. *Science with Young Children.* Washington, D.C.: NAEYC, 1977.

Holt, John. *How Children Learn*. New York: Pitman Publishing, 1964.

Holt, John. *How Children Learn*. New York: Pitman Publishing, 1967.

Nuffield Mathematics Project. *I Do, and I Understand*. New York: Wiley, 1967.

Pitcher, Evelyn, et al. *Helping Young Children Learn*. Columbus, Ohio: Charles E. Merrill, 1966.

Read, Katherine. *The Nursery School: Human Relationships and Learning*, 6th ed. Philadelphia: Saunders, 1976.

Rounds, Susan. *Teaching the Young Child*. New York: Agathon Press, 1975.

Seefeldt, Carol. *Curriculum for the Preschool-Primary Child: A Review of the Research*. Columbus, Ohio: Charles E. Merrill, 1976.

Seefeldt, Carol. *Social Studies for the Preschool-Primary Child*. Columbus, Ohio: Charles E. Merrill, 1977.

Sharp, Evelyn. *Thinking is Child's Play*. New York: Dutton, 1969.

Spodek, Bernard (Ed.) *Play: The Child Strives Toward Self-Actualization*. Washington, D. C.: NAEYC, 1971.

Spodek, Bernard. *Teaching in the Early Years*. Englewood Cliffs, N.J.: Prentice-Hall, Inc. 1972.

Sponseller, Doris (Ed.). *Play as a Learning Medium*. Washington, D. C.: NAEYC, 1974.

Van Allen, Roach. *Language Experiences in Communication*. Boston: Houghton Mifflin, 1976.

Yardley, Alice. *Senses and Sensitivity*. New York: Citation Press, 1973.

SELF-ASSESSMENT

After you have completed the reading, activities and small-group discussions, look again at the chapter objectives. Write a short paper responding to the following questions.

1. How would you describe your awareness, knowledge, and skill regarding the subject matter of this chapter before you began reading it and doing the activities?

2. To what extent do you feel that you have achieved each of the objectives presented at the beginning of the chapter?

3. What do you see as your strengths in this area?

4. In what specific areas do you need more information and experience? What kinds?

9

Working with Parents

PURPOSE AND OBJECTIVES

This chapter focuses on the importance of parent involvement in early childhood programs. In it, we discuss the role of parents in the child's development and some of the ways that teachers and parents can work together for the benefit of the child. Specifically, the objectives for this chapter are that you:

1. Become aware of the importance of parent involvement.
2. Become aware of your feelings and values about parent involvement.
3. Know some basic understandings and skills that will help you to work with parents.
4. Know three basic areas of parent involvement and some ways to implement each one.
5. Begin to develop skill in communicating with parents.

WORKING WITH PARENTS

It is challenging and demanding to discover how children develop, and to create learning experiences to support their growth. You, as a prospective teacher, need also to see each child as a part of a unique family situation in which the parents are his first and most important teachers and to realize that each child comes to school wrapped in the values, attitudes, and behaviors of his family. An important part of your developing skill as a teacher will be to learn to build relationships with parents that will help home and school work together to enhance the child's development.

Relating to parents has its own unique challenges and demands though some of what you will need to work successfully with parents will not be entirely new to you. The abilities that you have begun to develop in your work with children will be helpful with parents as well. It is not necessary to become intimate friends with parents, nor do you need to be the ultimate authority on child rearing. What you have to offer parents is a sense of yourself as a knowledgeable professional who is able to build a relationship and engage with them in supporting their child's development.

Dealing with parents may be gratifying as you develop warm relationships with them. It may also present some difficulties for you as a beginning teacher, especially if you are younger than many of the parents or if you have not had your own children. Some teachers find working with parents more threatening than working with children because they feel that parents are more likely than children to judge them negatively.

Just as you looked at your values and attitudes about working with children, you will want to examine your values regarding the involvement of parents in the early childhood program. You will also want to explore your attitudes about child rearing and see if you can allow for a variety of approaches that reflect differences in values, culture, and life-style. It is very likely that you will encounter differences in values about education and about child rearing with some of the parents that you will meet, and you will want to be aware of your own feelings about these differences and prepared to deal with them in constructive ways.

It will be helpful if, in the course of your training, you have experiences which provide you with opportunities to look at these issues and develop skills in relating to parents. Whenever possible you should arrange to attend parent meetings, to sit in on teacher-parent conferences, to visit children's homes, and in other ways gather firsthand experience of the children's families and the ways in which teachers of young children interact with parents. This chapter presents some ways to think about your relationships with parents and to begin in this very important aspect of your future role.

In this section we will look at some of the understandings and skills that provide the foundation for the teacher's work with parents. You have begun to develop some of these in your work with children, including understanding of child development, knowledge of early childhood programs, and communication skills.

Understandings and Skills Needed to Work with Parents

Understanding of Child Development

Your knowledge of child development influences your relationships with children and the kind of program you design for them. In working with children you use child development theory as a basis for decision making and planning. Knowledge of child development is also very important in your work with parents. With parents you need the ability to choose the important aspects of child development theory and communicate them clearly in ways which will enhance their understanding of their children and the school's program.

Your knowledge of children and child development establishes your role as a professional with something meaningful to share and allows you and the parent to meet each other on equal ground. Each of you brings to the interaction specialized information that will contribute to your ability to understand and work with the child. The parent brings knowledge of his child as a unique human being, and you bring your general knowledge of children.

Understanding of Early Childhood Programs

When your program decisions are based on knowledge about children, about curriculum, and on clear value choices, you will be comfortable with what you are doing and able to explain your rationale to others. Your clarity about your methods and their implications as well as your awareness of the alternatives can be communicated to parents. As parents observe your approach to curriculum and classroom management and listen to your rationale for what you do, they will learn more about children's development and become more aware of their own values and feelings about what constitutes desirable practice in teaching and relating to children.

Knowledge of What Parenting Is Like

Every parent is an individual with unique history, attitudes, values, and personal style. It is important to keep in mind that there are differences among parents while at the same time realizing that there are some experiences that are shared by most parents in our society.

Your work with parents will be enhanced by your awareness of their needs and problems and sensitivity to what parenting is like. It is easier to be sympathetic and supportive when you realize that being a parent in today's society is not an easy task. It involves a total, day-in-day-out responsibility that is unrelenting and cannot be ignored or avoided.

One reason for the difficulty that parents encounter is that society's view of their role has changed over the last several decades. It used to be enough to feed and clothe children and to insure their physical well-being. Today we are aware of the importance of the early years, and parents are told that they need specialized skills to aid in their children's development.

Methods of child rearing have changed since today's parents were children. Strict discipline or total permissiveness have given way to a number of different and often contradictory approaches. Learning about these approaches and choosing those which are consistent with an individual's values and personal style is a complex process.

And finally, the very structure of the family and its role has been changing over the last few generations. The purpose of the family has changed from the performance of specific survival functions and traditional roles of father as provider and mother as homemaker to more abstract tasks of providing psychological security and values to guide actions.

These changes in the nature of parenting require new skills and responses which many parents are not prepared for. Parents may find it confusing and difficult to find out the skills they need and the resources for acquiring them. They often find that they are forced to rely on social agencies, including schools, to perform many of the roles that were once the responsibility of the extended family. Part of your job as a teacher is to create relationships with parents which help them feel easier about sharing the responsibility for their child with you and turning to you for assistance.

Skills in Facilitating Relationships

The skills in communication and relationships that you have begun to develop in your work with children will be very applicable to your work with parents. Most people, adults and children, slowly develop new ideas and behavior patterns out of old responses. All people learn best in an atmosphere of concern, acceptance, and individualized attention. Parents, too, need to be seen as competent, well-intentioned, and capable of learning new things.

The basic communication skills of active listening and I-messages will also be helpful in communicating with parents. Begin by really listening and responding to feelings as well as words. When your needs are not being met, an I-message will convey your feelings without making parents feel that they are wrong. Let parents know the effect on you when they pick up their child an hour late or forget to send lunch or a change of clothes.

You will want to convey to parents that you have a commitment to hear their concerns and that you will face problems rather than avoiding them or insisting on your own solution. At times you will have differences which involve parents wanting you to teach or relate to their child in ways that are not comfortable for you; for example, wanting you to teach reading or math skills in preparation for the child's next grade in school. When this happens, it will require a delicate balancing act on your part to communicate to parents that you respect them and are willing to respond to their concerns and yet not to violate what you believe to be good for children.

It may be difficult to feel accepting of parents whose goals for children and ways of dealing with them are very different than yours. Moreover, you chose to be a teacher because of your allegiance to children, and it may be hard to feel good about a parent who doesn't seem to care, or even abuses a young child. You need to keep in mind that parenting is difficult, that there are few resources available, and that the great majority of parents *are* trying to do the best they can given their circumstances.

In many cases the school is the most accessible and most comfortable place for parents to go to share personal concerns and problems and to get help in dealing with their children. If you can communicate your awareness of the difficulty of the parent role and your genuine interest and concern, you may become a valuable source of support for the family.

Areas of Teacher-Parent Interaction in Early Childhood Programs

The first major area of teacher-parent interaction is communicating and sharing information about the child and the program. In order for home and school to work together, it is essential that teachers give careful thought and attention to developing regular communication with parents.

Parent education is the second area of teacher-parent interaction. Through parent education, teachers contribute to the quality of the parent-child relationship. Parent education will vary according to the type of program, parent interest, and teacher skill and commitment to the process.

The third major area of teacher-parent interaction is the involvement of parents in the school program. Involvement in the school can provide an opportunity for parents to grow in competence, contributes to the school program, and provides many opportunities for parents and teachers to cooperate. The amount of actual parent involvement in the classroom and school will vary with the amount of time and interest that parents show and with the teacher's skill and commitment. The kind of program you teach in will be an important factor in determining the extent of this kind of involvement. Parent

cooperative schools are based on regular parent participation in the classroom, while full-day programs for working parents obviously cannot expect the same amount of participation in the daily program.

Your knowledge of children and of early childhood programs, combined with respect for the nature of parenting and commitment to increasing the quality of relationships, will contribute to your ability to relate effectively and constructively to parents in these three areas. It is best to begin involving parents in your program by finding out some things about them—their needs, concerns, the level of their interest, amount of time they are able to participate, and the kinds of activities they prefer to participate in. It may be helpful to have parents fill out a form giving some of this information when they first enter their child in school. It will also be important to your success if you involve parents in the planning process.

"Parent participation cannot be a preconceived structure into which the parent group is placed. It begins as parents and staff examine, clarify and harmonize expectations of each other" (Adair and Eckstein, 1969, p. 7).

Communicating with Parents

The first interaction you have with parents may be to help them to decide if your program is the right one for their child and family. You can aid this process by open exchange of information—the parents will let you know what their child is like and what kind of program they want for him, and you will tell them about your program, your teaching philosophy, and possibly about alternatives to your program.

Once the family has chosen to send its child to your school, you may want to begin developing a relationship by having a meeting to introduce new parents to the school and its expectations; you can learn of their interests, concerns, and expectations. You might also find it valuable to visit the home before the child enters school to get acquainted individually.

The way you handle the first day of school will be important in shaping parents' impressions of you and their ideas about what kind of relationship they can expect to have with you. The child's entrance to the school setting need not be difficult if it has been carefully planned and if you realize that separation can be quite traumatic for some parents as well as some children. It may help in this initial adjustment if you have met the child before he comes to school the first day, if you have gathered information that may make the separation easier, and if you have designed procedures to make entrance to school pleasant and comfortable. Some procedures that may be helpful are to:

- Have a staggered schedule for entering children so that only a few come each day for the first week.

- Invite parents to come with their child the first day (possibly inviting parents to another room for a meeting or for coffee so the child can become used to their absence).

- Introduce each child individually to the school setting

so he has the information he needs to find his way and to know that his needs will be met.

- Invite the child to bring a special object like a toy or blanket that may be comforting and serve as a link between home and school.

What is most important is that you respect the feelings of both parent and child, that you are reassuring, and communicate your confidence that the child will be able to adjust to the new setting.

Because of their previous experiences with schools, parents may not feel comfortable in their initial contacts with you so you may need to assume responsibility, in the beginning, for building a relationship of trust. In order to keep parents informed, you will want to share information regularly about the school's activities, how the child is adjusting, and what you have observed about his development. Remember to share your good feelings as well as your concerns about the child.

Creative planning is important in developing good communication with parents. Some effective ways of sharing information include: newsletters, bulletin boards, telephone calls, informal gatherings like picnics and potluck suppers, home visits, informal chats when the child is dropped off or picked up at school, and scheduled parent conferences. Whenever possible, include parents in the planning of social events and in the writing of newsletters and other communications.

Keeping in contact with busy working parents may involve having a staff member responsible for greeting parents at the times when children enter and leave school, arranging phone conferences, and other channels for communication, like suggestion boxes and envelopes for messages to parents and to staff.

Another good way to communicate with parents is to create a parent corner near the entrance to the school where new materials are displayed regularly. This area might have coffee or tea available as well as books, articles, pictures of the children, samples of activities, and even a slide/tape presentation portraying aspects of your program.

Parent conferences are useful in that they provide parents and teachers with a block of time during which they can share their perceptions of the child's development and problem solve in areas of concern. Parent conferences provide a more in-depth exchange of information. During a parent conference, you may explore issues relating to the parents' relationship with their child, and parents may share some of their personal problems. Your role in this kind of interaction is to help parents express and clarify their feelings and values, give information, and help them develop their own skills and resources. You may find at times that you don't have the energy or skill to handle a problem. You will want to be aware of resources in the community such as parenting courses, child guidance clinics, and psychological services, in order to make appropriate referrals when needed.

Parent Education

Parent education involves helping parents understand that they have a tremendously important role in their child's development—that they are, in fact, their child's first and most important teacher, and that the way the child learns to speak, think, and feel about himself and others is significantly influenced by the kinds of relationships he has with his parents in infancy and early childhood.

Your role as a teacher is to help parents understand their child, to understand how they influence their child's development and how their child influences them, and to develop skills in parenting consistent with their values.

It is important that whatever you do in the area of parent involvement be based on clearly identified values and a consistent philosophy. Evelyn Pickarts and Jean Fargo in their book *Parent Education* (1971) urge teachers to work with parents in ways that allow for individual choice and personal development. They see the role of the teacher as helping parents to increase in compassion, competence, and individual autonomy.

> Most parents will not come knocking at your door to demand an education program. Many of them do not perceive themselves serving an important role as teachers of their own children, and they rarely have access to information

suggesting what they can do. You can develop interest by planning as carefully for and with parents as you do in the case of children [Nedler, 1977, p. 129].

Parent education can take place in many ways. Informally, it occurs as the teacher models behaviors that contribute to the development of children and converses with parents in the course of their regular contacts. Formally, it can take place through newsletters, workshops, parent discussion groups, and courses in parenting skills.

Parent Involvement in the Program

The third important role that you will play with parents is that of encouraging and supporting their participation in your program. Teachers need parents because the active, involved, concerned parent can function as a member of the teaching team, enriching experiences for the children and freeing the teacher for more individual interaction; support curriculum experiences, aiding the teacher to enlarge the learning environment into the community; supplement parent involvement through orienting other parents to classroom participation and philosophy; and provide input into school management and strengthen the community relatedness of the entire program. The values in having parents as part of the teaching team can be threefold:

For the parents:

- Observation and participation in their child's program offers an opportunity to learn the teacher's way of relating to children and alternative ways of guiding growth and development;

- gain firsthand insight into the meaning of the curriculum for their children's learning and tools for implementing this growth at home;

- develop a sense of competence in being a needed and increasingly contributing part of the program;

- develop relationships with other parents in the community.

For the children:

- A chance to see their own parents in a different role;

- an opportunity to relate to many different adults with different skills, feelings, and ways of relating;

- more individualized attention and a teacher freer to meet their individual needs;

- a richer curriculum because of parents' contributions.

For the teacher:

- A chance to expand the program because of increased staff;

- an opportunity to observe the relationship between parent and child;

- a more meaningful relationship with parents because of the experience of working together;

- a chance to contribute to the competence of parents who through this experience move into new types of growth and involvement in the community;

- a chance to reach parents who are not yet involved because they have more time and the help of parents.

Involving parents in the daily program takes some additional skills and planning, but the results in terms of enriching the program for children and providing opportunities for teachers and parents to work together are well worth it. As a beginning teacher, you may want to plan parent involvement in your classroom in easy stages until it becomes comfortable for you and the parents.

There are many ways that parents can become involved in the educational program, including observation of their child in the classroom, visits to the school for special occasions, assistance during field trips, and working with children in the classroom. It is important that parents be able to participate in ways that feel comfortable and natural to them and that they be offered support in developing skills for each new kind of involvement. Special efforts may be needed to insure that fathers as well as mothers participate since men often feel that the early childhood program is not their natural province.

Cooperative planning will do a great deal to set the stage for satisfying experiences for the parents. An orientation period before school starts will help parents to feel prepared and to learn classroom routines. A card file which contains information about activities and jobs that need to be done is useful for letting parents know what kinds of participation will be welcomed. Posting written directions in each area of the classroom describing the purpose of the activities and how adults can interact with children in that area is another good technique for supporting participation. An opportunity for parents and teachers to meet together and discuss the day's events allows them to share experiences and give each other feedback.

A parent who does not have time or who is uncomfortable participating in the classroom regularly may enjoy making educational materials at home or coming to school for an occasional clean-up or renovation. Another way to involve parents is to invite them to share some unique skill or knowledge like a cultural celebration, a story, a craft, or a special recipe.

Parent involvement in decision making can help your program more accurately reflect the interests and needs of the families that you serve. Parents may enhance a program's effectiveness by making suggestions and by serving on advisory or policy making boards.

The way that teachers view home-school relationships can range from contacting parents only when there is a problem to perceiving the school as a center for serving the needs of families. The nature of parent involvement in your program should reflect the children's needs, the parents values and needs, and your values and needs. Open communication and cooperation between parents and teachers hold the greatest potential for accomplishing their common task of helping the child grow into an independent, resourceful person.

REFERENCES

Adair, Thelma, and Eckstein, Esther. *Parents and the Day Care Center.* New York: Federation of Protestant Welfare Agencies, Inc., 1969.

Bromberg, Susan. "A Beginning Teacher Works with Parents." *Young Children,* December 1968.

Coletta, Anthony. *Working Together: A Guide to Parent Involvement.* Georgia: Humanics Limited, 1977.

Gordon, Thomas. *T.E.T.—Teacher Effectiveness Training.* New York: David McKay Co., 1974.

Honig, Alice. *Parent Involvement in Early Childhood Education.* Washington, D.C.: NAEYC, 1975.

Nedler, Shari. "Working with Parents on the Run." *Childhood Education,* January 1977.

Pickarts, Evelyn, and Fargo, Jean. *Parent Education: Toward Parental Competence.* New York: Appleton-Century-Crofts, 1971.

Simmons-Martin, Audrey. "Facilitating Parent-Child Interactions through the Education of Parents." *Journal of Research and Development in Education,* Winter 1975.

Stevens, Joseph, and King, Edith. *Administering Early Childhood Programs.* Boston: Little, Brown and Co., 1976.

Wilson, Gary. *Parents and Teachers: Humanistic Educational Techniques to Facilitate Communication between Parents and Staff of Education Programs.* Georgia: Humanics Limited, 1974.

ACTIVITIES

Report on the activities assigned by:

1. Writing a 3–5 page reaction paper.
2. Using another medium (tape, photography, drawing, etc.) with the instructor's consent.

1. Observe an early childhood program for evidence of parental involvement. Describe your impressions of the amount and kinds of parent-teacher communication, parent education, parent participation in the classroom and in the school decision making. What seems to be the staff's attitudes and values regarding work with parents? Do you feel they are committed to a close home-school relationship?

2. Attend a meeting in which parents and teachers are interacting (a conference, school social function, etc.). Describe your impressions of the nature of the teacher-parent relationships. What kind of information is exchanged about the children and the program?

3. As a future teacher, explore your thoughts and feelings about working with parents. Will you feel as comfortable working with parents as you would with children? Why or why not? Do you feel you have the necessary skills for working successfully with parents? If you believe not, what will you do about it?

4. Write an imaginary dialogue between a teacher and a parent
   —whose child is reluctant to go to school;
   or
   —whose child has recently been biting other children;
   or
   —who is resentful of an ex-spouse's failure to cooperate in parenting;
   or
   —use a problem you have encountered.

5. If these activities do not challenge you design your own activity with the consent of the instructor.

DISCUSSION GUIDE

1. Share any ways you recall that your parents participated in your early school experiences. What do you believe the school's attitude was regarding the role of parents in the education of young children?

2. Choose an early childhood program you have observed and share your perceptions regarding the school's values and attitudes concerning the involvement of parents. What kinds of parent participation did you observe?

3. What is your attitude about the role of parents in schools? What do you see as your potential strengths and weaknesses in working with parents? What additional understandings and skills do you feel you will need to work effectively with parents?

4. What kinds of parents might you feel most comfortable interacting with? Are there parents you would be unable to work with? What are the implications for you of this awareness?

RESOURCES

Adair, Thelma, and Eckstein, Esther. *Parents and the Day Care Center.* New York: Federation of Protestant Welfare Agencies, Inc., 1969.

Bromberg, Susan. "A Beginning Teacher Works with Parents." *Young Children,* December 1968.

Coletta, Anthony J. *Working Together: A Guide to Parent Involvement.* Georgia: Humanics Limited, 1977.

Crocker, Eleanor Cartwright. "Depth Consultation with Parents." *Young Children,* November 1964.

Gordon, Thomas. *Teacher Effectiveness Training.* New York: David McKay Co., 1974.

Greenberg, Polly. "Seminars in Parenting Preschoolers." *Early Childhood Education: It's an Art? It's a Science?,* edited by J. D. Andrews. Washington, D.C.: NAEYC, 1976.

Hess, Robert, and Croft, Doreen. *Teachers of Young Children.* New York: Houghton Mifflin Co., 1972.

Hildebrand, Verna. *Guiding Young Children.* New York: MacMillan, 1975.

Honig, Alice. *Parent Involvement in Early Childhood Education.* Washington, D.C.: NAEYC, 1975.

Nedler, Shari. "Working with Parents on the Run." *Childhood Education,* January 1977.

Pickarts, Evelyn, and Fargo, Jean. *Parent Education: Toward Parental Competence.* New York: Appleton-Century-Crofts, 1971.

Read, Katherine. *The Nursery School,* 6th ed. Philadelphia: W. B. Saunders, 1976.

Stevens, Joseph, and King, Edith. *Administering Early Childhood Programs.* Boston: Little, Brown and Co., 1976.

Wilson, Gary. *Parents and Teachers: Humanistic Educational Techniques to Facilitate Communication Between Parents and Staff of Educational Programs.* Georgia: Humanics Limited, 1974.

SELF-ASSESSMENT

After you have completed the reading, activities, and small-group discussions, look again at the chapter objectives. Write a short paper responding to the following questions.

1. How would you describe your awareness, knowledge, and skill regarding the subject matter of this chapter before you began reading it and doing the activities?

2. To what extent do you feel that you have achieved each of the objectives presented at the beginning of the chapter?

3. What do you see as your strengths in this area?

4. In what specific areas do you need more information and experience? What kinds?

Postscript

We would like to use this postscript to share with you some of the ideas and advice that our students have found helpful to them when they began to teach. We know of no way that you can be truly prepared for the real world of teaching. No matter how much experience you get in working with children in the course of your training, there is nothing that compares to the day-to-day experience of having full responsibility for a group of young children.

Another reason that you may feel unprepared for what you may encounter when you begin to teach is that many teacher education programs prepare you to work in schools as education professors would like them to be and not necessarily as they really are. They do this because they feel that the responsibility of a training program is to prepare its students to provide the best possible experiences for young children.

Our experience has led us to believe that it is important to pay attention not only to the development of the whole child, but to the whole teacher as well. Attention to the teacher's intellectual, physical, social, and emotional development may be very important in her success in teaching.

The first year of teaching is difficult. Lilian Katz (1972) describes it as the "survival" stage in which the teacher's main concern is whether she can make it through the next day, week, or month. At this stage in a teacher's development, a support system is helpful. Relationships with colleagues can often provide encouragement, resources, and moral support. It is also nice to have a special friend—perhaps another beginning teacher—with whom you can share your joys and sorrows.

During your first year of teaching it may be almost enough intellectual stimulation to absorb and apply what you learned in your teacher education program. If it is available, on-site consultation focused on specific problems is the most appropriate form of training for the beginning teacher (Katz, 1972). You might also enjoy joining a professional organization of early childhood educators like a local affiliate group of the National Association for the Education of Young Children (NAEYC), or the Association for Childhood Education International (ACEI). These and other organizations will bring you into contact with other teachers and provide workshops with practical ideas for teaching.

Early childhood educators are careful to pay attention to the health, nutrition, and physical development of children but have tended to overlook these very important areas for teachers. Yet, without physical stamina, good health, and a good diet, a teacher is not adequately prepared for the strenuous activity required to work with children for long hours every day.

Buhler and Aspy have conducted studies which point to the direct relationship between a teacher's physical fitness and the quality of her relationships with children. They have, in fact, found that teachers who are physically fit tend to run more humane classrooms than teachers who are not (Buhler et al., 1975, p. 122).

Daniel Jordan (1973) points out the importance of the teacher's diet and suggests, for example, that deficiency of B vitamins can lead to reduced ability to deal with stress and handle anxiety.

As a beginning teacher, you will be doing a great service to yourself and to the children you teach if you pay special attention to your own health and physical fitness, including a balanced diet (especially a good breakfast), regular exercise, and opportunity to quiet your body and mind through some form of relaxation like yoga or meditation.

One of the recurring problems in the emotional development of beginning teachers is that they often have unrealistically high expectations of themselves and expect to achieve instant perfection. Remember that the first year in any new job is difficult and that teaching young children is a complex and demanding responsibility. No one is expected to get it all together and be a superlative teacher in the first year. It may be helpful to set minimum goals and work on one area of your teaching at a time, rather than trying to accomplish everything at once. In this way you are more likely to see some tangible accomplishments.

The order of presentation of this book may give some suggestions on how to establish your priorities. You will probably want to begin by focusing on your relationships with the children, next on making the environment work, then on designing learning experiences, and finally on working with parents. Of course, you cannot ignore any of these areas, but you can choose where you will place your emphasis. You may find at first that you will have to improvise in some areas with whatever energy you can muster.

It is important to remember when you begin teaching that, like the children, you are a person in the process of development. If you apply the same developmental perspective to yourself that you do to children, you may be able to appreciate your own growth in terms of where you started from and not condemn yourself for what you see as shortcomings and failures.

An important part of your ongoing developmental process will be to learn to use feedback constructively. When other people share their responses (both positive and negative) to you and your teaching, it gives you valuable insight into the impact you have on others and how they see you as a teacher. Negative feedback need not be regarded as criticism, which calls for justification and defensiveness; rather, it gives you information you need to evaluate your own development and to know which areas you need to work on.

Our greatest wish for you is that you will remain open to new ideas and experiences; that you will be flexible; that you will really listen to the thoughts of others, weigh new information, and make teaching choices in terms of the long-range good for children and not from your attachment to one point of view or to one way of doing things. Teaching, like living, is a process of constant growth and change. If you keep this in mind, you will keep growing and changing, becoming progressively better able to support the development of young children.

REFERENCES

Buhler, June H., Roebuck, Flora, and Brookshire, William. "The Relationship between the Physical Fitness of a Selected Sample of Student Teachers and Their Performances on Flanders' Interaction Analysis Categories." In *Physical Health for Educators,* June H. Buhler and David N. Aspy (Eds.). Denton, Texas: North Texas State University, 1975.

Jordan, Daniel C., and Streets, Donald T. "The Anisa Model: A New Basis for Educational Planning." *Young Children.* Washington, D.C.: NAEYC, June 1973, pp. 290–307.

Katz, Lilian G. "Developmental Stages of Preschool Teachers." *The Elementary School Journal,* 1972, 23(1), pp. 50–54.

Index